A Supplementary Edition

of

A History

of

Greenup County

Kentucky

Compiled by:
Nina Mitchell Biggs

Southern Historical Press, Inc.
Greenville, South Carolina

Please Direct All Correspondence and Book Orders to:

Southern Historical Press, Inc.
1071 Park West Blvd.
Greenville, SC   29611

Originally printed: KY 1962
ISBN #978-1-63914-608-6
Printed in the United States of America

This Supplementary Edition
of
A History of Greenup County
is dedicated to the memory
of its pioneers and to their
descendants.

In the beginning God created the heaven and the earth. Genesis 1:1.

And after eons of time a small part of His earth became Kentucky, of which Greenup County is a part.

Foreword

THREE HUNDRED copies of *A History of Greenup County* came from the Franklin Press of Louisville, Kentucky, May, 1951, and all were sold before the end of the year. Two hundred copies, with a few changes made, were printed May, 1952, and very few remain in the hands of the authors.

Since the printing of the two histories, we have received much interesting material and feel encouraged to have a limited number of copies of *A Supplementary Edition of A History of Greenup County* printed, which will be a smaller and cheaper book than the earlier ones. For the benefit of those who do not have one of the first printing and may purchase one of the last, we have included a history of the formation of the county and an early plotting of the county seat with lists of officials as contained in the other books.

We have received many letters from people asking for information of ancestry and have replied to the best of our knowledge. We have had some interesting experiences with readers of the history, among them two sons of teachers of the 1870's and 1880's, G. B. Norris (Bert), son of Professor J. B. Norris, of Columbus, Ohio, and Henry Kenyon, son of S. T. Kenyon, both of whom were too young to attend school. The first lives at Columbus, Ohio, and visits Greenup occasionally; the other at St. Cloud, Florida, where he grows fruit for his family and friends. We have had interesting visitors, among them a family from southwestern Kentucky, named Greenup, who on a tour through Virginia, passed through Greenup County and came to ask if Governor Christopher Greenup had lived in the County. He told us that his people were relatives of the governor in Virginia. Another visitor, traveling by bus to Florida, and having seen *A History of Greenup County* at Winchester, Kentucky, came off his route and walked the long lane to get a copy. When he asked and was told the price, he said he was not prepared to pay that much, and was turning to leave. We asked what he would like to pay, and he went away with a copy. We have realized there were others like him, which is a reason for the printing of a less expensive book.

Appreciation is due Mr. George Corum for the interest shown in the production of pictures contained in this book.

We hope this Supplementary Edition will be received by our readers in the same kindly spirit in which it is written.

THE AUTHOR

NOTE: The author regrets that her co-author, Mabel Lace Mackoy, is not with her in the compilation of this edition.

Contents

A Supplementary Edition

of

A History of Greenup County

NORTH

OHIO

Scioto R.

Portsmouth, Ohio

MAP OF
GREENUP
COUNTY
1860

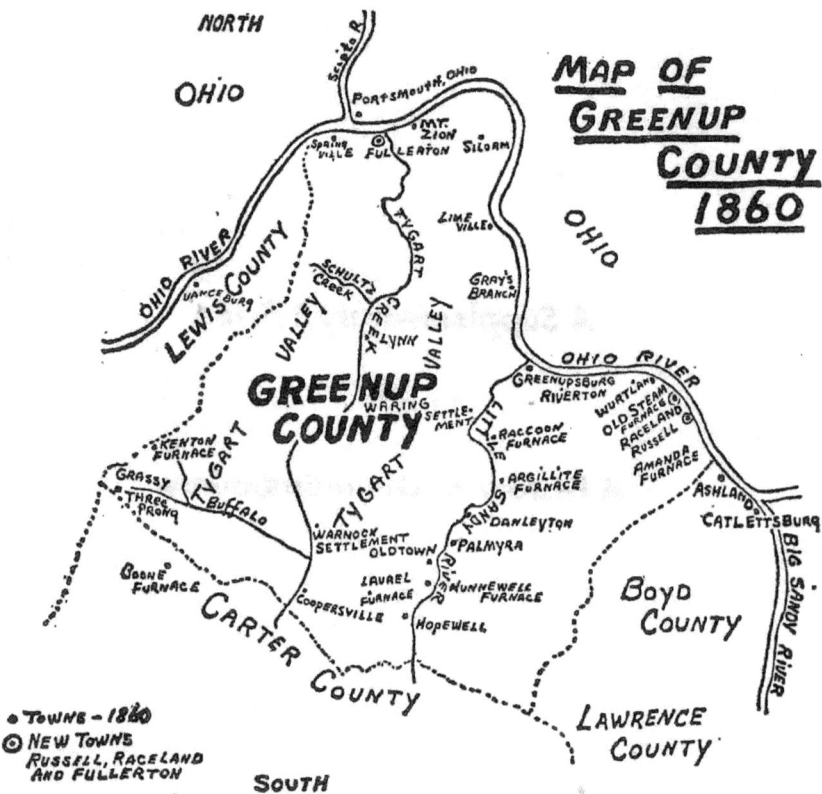

Spring Ville

Fullerton

MT. ZION

Siloam

Lime Ville

TYGART

OHIO

Schultz Creek

CREEK

LYNN

Gray's Branch

TYGART VALLEY

VANCEBURG

LEWIS COUNTY

OHIO RIVER

Greenupsburg

OHIO RIVER

Riverton

Wurtland

Old Steam Furnace

Raceland

Russell

GREENUP
COUNTY

WARING SETTLEMENT

Raccoon Furnace

TYGART VALLEY

KENTON FURNACE

Grassy

Three Prong

Buffalo

Warnock Settlement

Oldtown

Argillite Furnace

Amanda Furnace

ASHLAND

CATLETTSBURG

SANDY

Danleyton

Palmyra

Laurel Furnace

Coopersville

Nunnewell Furnace

Hopewell

BOYD COUNTY

BIG SANDY RIVER

Boone Furnace

CARTER COUNTY

LAWRENCE COUNTY

SOUTH

Towns - 1860
New Towns
Russell, Raceland
and Fullerton

I

Greenup County

GREENUP COUNTY was formed June, 1803 from Mason County. It extended from the Mason County line to the Big Sandy River, a distance of forty miles along the Ohio River, and with an average width of twelve miles. From a part of this area four counties have been formed, Lewis (1806), Lawrence (1821), Carter (1838), and Boyd (1860). The last named occupied the most northeasterly section of the state.

The County was named for Christopher Greenup who was born in Virginia in 1750, fought in the French and Indian War, and was a colonel in the Revolutionary War. He became very prominent in the organization of the state of Kentucky, occupied several important offices, and was elected governor of the state in 1804.

The earliest settlers were mostly farmers and corn was the principal crop with wheat next. Some grist mills were constructed on the banks of Little Sandy River and on Tygart Creek. With plenty of all sorts of trees, sawmills were soon making lumber for building. With clay at hand, it was not long until bricks were made and buildings constructed. The hills were found to contain many kinds of minerals, and with stone at hand, blast furnaces were built, one as early as 1818, and by 1857 there were eleven in operation. There were also two iron foundries, three flour mills, and several lumber mills. The last two were usually operated as one. Before 1860 when Boyd County was formed from Greenup, the county population was 8,700, and that of Boyd was 6,044. The population of Ashland in 1870 was 1,479, and that of Catlettsburg was 1,019, while Greenupsburg numbered but 507. The population of Greenup in the 1850 census numbered 1,200. Springville (South Portsmouth) in 1870 had a population of 250, Lynn in 1846 was noted for its shoemakers and tanners. In 1850, Riverton had a population of about 50. Above this, many of the pioneer farms are now occupied by industrial plants. The old village of

Wurtland has grown into a town, and the new towns of Raceland, Worthington and Flatwoods have come into existence due to the Chesapeake and Ohio Railroad.

Settlement

More than one hundred and seventy-five years had elapsed from the settlement of Virginia in 1607 to the close of the Revolutionary War in 1783. The state had become pretty well settled and the best lands had been taken. Adventurers and traders were bringing back to Virginia tales of the new land of Kentucky, of its many rivers, forests and prairie lands and to many it became "the Promised Land."

After the close of the war "grants of land" were given to the men who had served in it in proportion to services rendered by them. Many took advantage of these, and many settlers came in the latter 1770's and the 1780's. Kentucky was made a state in 1792. Some of the settlers came overland, following the windings of the rivers, some through a pass later called Cumberland Gap, while many others came to the head of the Ohio River, where flatboats were built, and came down the river with their families and household necessities.

Many of those who came down the river settled on its banks, while others made their way up the small streams, which in Greenup County were the Little Sandy River and Tygart Creek. Oak, pine, poplar, beech, chestnut and hickory trees provided abundant material for building purposes. In the hills were plenty of coal for fuel, stone, iron ore and other minerals.

The county of Greenup was formed in 1803 and was named for Governor Christopher Greenup, who was born in Virginia in 1750, fought in the wars against the Indians, and was a colonel in the Revolutionary War. He was prominent in the organization of the District of Kentucky, a member of the first Congress, and became governor in 1804.

Settlers

Thomas Waring, Jesse Boone, Seriah Stratton, Andrew and Thomas Hood were the men instrumental in the forming of Greenup County and of the town of Greenupsburg. These men met in the home of Andrew Hood to plan the organization of the county and the "Platting" of the town. In May, 1804, they met in the Hood home to form a circuit court.

Thomas Waring had come from Maryland to Mason County and from there to the new county, where he purchased one thousand acres of land on Tygart Creek from the government. This became known as the Waring Settlement. Jesse Boone came from North Carolina and became owner of a great deal of land above Town Branch. He was active in all the early affairs of the county, aiding in the organization of courts. He was an associate judge with Thomas Waring, was the third postmaster, and was succeeded by his son, Alphonse. Seriah Stratton came from Mason County and became a resident of the town. He was an associate justice. We do not know a great deal about the family. Ann Stratton married Jacob Friend in 1808, Jane Stratton married Nelson Brown in 1810, and James Stratton married Elizabeth McGuire in 1815.

Andrew Hood was perhaps the first resident in the present limits of the county. He had come from Virginia with his family, after having fought in the French and Indian War and in the Revolutionary War in Virginia. His home was "two miles above the Little Sandy River." He was active in the organization of the county, the town, the courts, and the planning of roads. Thomas Hood, one of the "founders," was a member of the courts and was a member of the first jury.

Captain Moses Fuqua was a Revolutionary soldier in Virginia and obtained more than one thousand acres of land above the mouth and along the banks of Tygart Creek in 1799. Moses Jr. came to arrange a place for the family, and on returning home with his report the family came and settled on the bank of Tygart. Moses Jr. married soon after and lived in this home, where he reared a family of ten daughters and one son.

John and James Mackoy came from Campbell County, Virginia, about 1800. John had married Lavinia, daughter of Moses Fuqua, in Virginia. They settled on land at what is now Siloam. He was interested in all early affairs and one of the three men "to view the best way for a road to be built from the mouth of the Scioto River to the mouth of the Big Sandy." James Mackoy settled in Mason County, where he operated one of the first mills in that county.

Isaac Hockaday came from Virginia to Clark County, Kentucky, and from there to Greenup, perhaps to aid in its organization, in 1803. He served one year as county clerk, when he was succeeded by his son John. The Hockaday family lived above Town Branch, near the Boone and Hood lands, and later acquired a great deal of the land that had been owned by them.

Daniel Boone was at one time a resident at the Jesse Boone farm, but was not active in any of the early affairs of the county.

Greenupsburg in Early Days

Greenupsburg, as the town was named until 1880, when it became Greenup, was platted a short time after the county was organized, by the same men who had surveyed and organized the county. In 1815 a plat of the town, made earlier by Lewis Craig, was recorded in the Clerk's Office, which embraced that part lying between Town Branch on the east and the Little Sandy River on the west.

The town was laid off around a central square about halfway between the eastern and western sections. From the river to the hill the streets were named Water, Elizabeth, Main and Perry. The street east of the central square was named Harrison, and that west, Washington. The alleys from Harrison east were named Laurel and Hickory, and those on the west were Cedar, Walnut, and Cherry. The remaining land was known as Ferry Lot. Water Street soon became Front Street, and when the alleys were marked as streets in 1954, Boston Alley became Ash Street and the one above, became Jefferson Street.

All of the early meetings were held at the home of Andrew Hood. A log courthouse was built in 1806. A new one was begun in the center of the square in 1811 but was not finished until 1816. This was the square brick building that was in use until 1937 when it was badly damaged by the flood of that year. The present building was finished in 1939. The first Clerk's Office stood on the north side of the court square facing the river, and the jail on the south side facing Main Street. The new courthouse houses all county offices. The jail was razed and the present one erected at the corner of Elizabeth and Cedar Streets in 1900.

The Plat of Greenupsburg made by Lewis Craig shows that Lot No. 1 was at Water and Washington Streets and No. 11 at Ferry Lot. No. 12 began at the corner of Water and Harrison Streets, and the last lot, No. 23, was at Boston Alley. A wooden bridge was built very early connecting the town with that part lying east, and until a covered wooden bridge was built across Little Sandy, in the early 1850's, ferries were in use.

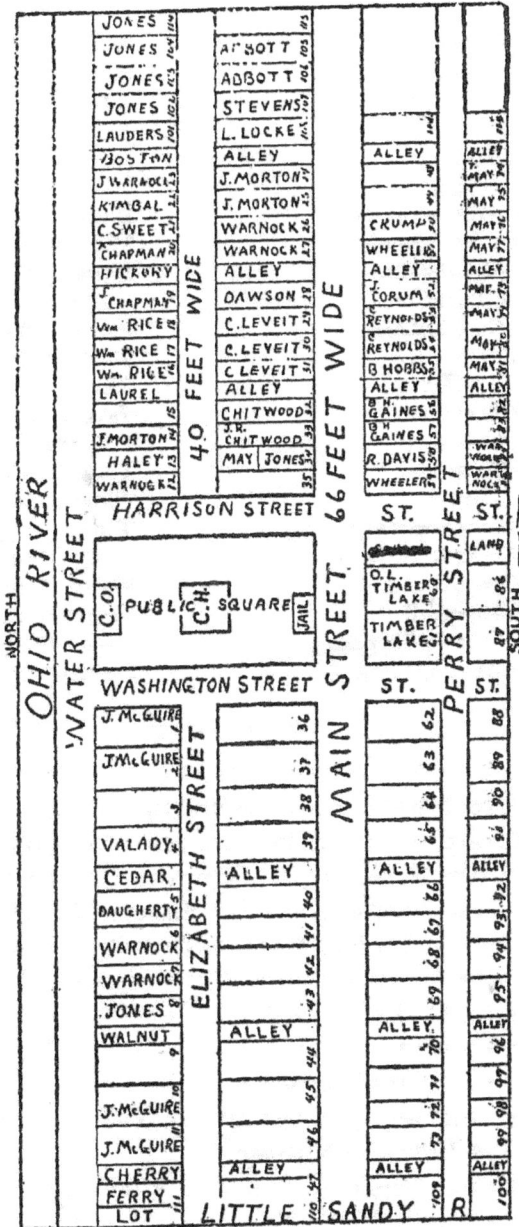

A PLAN OF THE TOWN OF GREENUPSBURG COPIED FROM THE SECOND YEAR BOOK

NORTH

OHIO RIVER

WATER STREET

JONES
JONES
JONES
JONES
LAUDERS
BOSTON
J. WARNOCK
KIMBAL
C. SWEET
CHAPMAN
HICKORY
CHAPMAN
Wm RICE
Wm RICE
Wm RICE
LAUREL
J. MORTON
HALEY
WARNOCK

40 FEET WIDE

ABBOTT
ADBOTT
STEVENS
L. LOCKE
ALLEY
J. MORTON
J. MORTON
WARNOCK
WARNOCK
ALLEY
DAWSON
C. LEVEIT
C. LEVEIT
C. LEVEIT
ALLEY
CHITWOOD
J.R. CHITWOOD
MAY JONES

66 FEET WIDE

ALLEY

CRUMP
WHEELING
ALLEY
CORUM
REYNOLDS
REYNOLDS
B HOBBS
ALLEY
G.H. GAINES
G.H. GAINES
R. DAVIS
WHEELER

ALLEY
MAY
MAY
MAY
MAY
ALLEY
MAY
MAY
MAY
MAY
ALLEY

WAR NOCK
WAR NOCK

HARRISON STREET   ST.   ST.

PUBLIC SQUARE
C.O.   C.H.   JAIL

O.L. TIMBERG LAKE

TIMBER LAKE

LAND

SOUTH

WASHINGTON STREET   ST.   ST.

J. McGUIRE
J. McGUIRE

VALADY
CEDAR
DAUGHERTY
WARNOCK
WARNOCK
JONES
WALNUT

J. McGUIRE
J. McGUIRE
CHERRY
FERRY LOT

ELIZABETH STREET

ALLEY

ALLEY

ALLEY

MAIN STREET

ALLEY

ALLEY

ALLEY

PERRY STREET

ALLEY

ALLEY

ALLEY

LITTLE SANDY R

Pioneers

Names and settlements of Greenup County other than the Census of 1810. When the new counties were formed from the large area, many names disappeared from Census of Greenup County:

Alberson—Siloam	Jacobs—Wurtland
Allen—Oldtown	Kendall—Oldtown
Anderson—White Oak	King—Kings
Bagby—Springville	Lee—Tygart
Baker—Tygart	Lybrooks—White Oak
Bennett—Tygart	Martin—Fulton Forge
Berkeley—Little Sandy	Mefford—Greenupsburg
Brammer—Wurtland	Merrill—Lime Kiln
Brooker—Springville	Moran—Greenup
Brooks—Liberty	Patterson—Fulton Forge
Burton—Coal Branch	Patton—Raccoon
Bush—Siloam	Rankins—Greenupsburg
Callihan—Palmyra	Stark—Oldtown
Clary—White Oak	Swearingin—Argillite
Clifton—Oldtown	Tanner—Greenupsburg
Collins—Wurtland	Taylor—Tygart
Cooper—Tygart	Thom—Tygart
Corum—Greenupsburg	Tinsley—Tygart
Doran—Short Branch	Tong—Lime Kiln
Eifort—Greenupsburg	Winn—Greenupsburg
Elam—Hunnewell	Wurts—Laurel Furnace
Fisher—Amanda Furnace	York—Greenupsburg
Hertel—Greenupsburg	Zuhars—Springville

Early Notes

From the *Greenupsburg Independent* of May 25, 1871, edited by George Creel, we take the following items:

Greenupsburg has eight lawyers and three physicians. (Names of these occur in *A History of Greenup County*.)

Cars are now running on the Eastern Kentucky Railroad to Hopewell, four miles beyond Hunnewell. The track will be laid to Pactolus in a few days and to Grayson about June 1st.

Governor R. H. Leslie and John M. Harland, Democratic and Republican Candidates for Governor of Kentucky, will address the citizens of Greenupsburg Friday June 2nd.

The following was printed in the *Independent*, having been taken from the *Franklin Sentinel*:

Greenupsburg, "the county seat of Greenup County is a beautiful town of about 800 inhabitants, with a bank, fireproof Clerk's Office, a Masonic Hall, three churches and nice homes. It has a weekly neutral newspaper published by George Creel, which is a very newsy paper."

Correction of Errors that Occurred in 1951 and 1952 Editions of *A History of Greenup County*

Nancy, wife of Martin Smith, is not buried in a little graveyard on the McClave farm near Limeville, but on the home farm by the side of her husband, above Riverton. Their graves are marked by headstones and are enclosed by a stone wall.

Vernon Taylor, who lost his life in the Spanish-American War in 1898, was son of Henry and Electa McGinness Taylor of Tygart Valley.

Nettie Johnson, Aura Cremeans and Lily Davis were daughters of Gilbert and Martha Taylor Nichols.

Vernon VanBibber married Edna Meadows.

In the Dupuy family, William Stevens should read William Stevenson.

In the Virgin family, Henry should read Harvey.

The Greenup Academy was built in 1815, on the corner of Harrison and Perry (not Main) Streets.

The old covered wooden bridge near the mouth of Little Sandy was constructed in the late 1840's or early 1850's instead of 1880 as printed.

Dr. Henry T. Morris received his M.D. in 1897, instead of 1879.

Anthony Thomson was born in 1789, instead of 1799.

Firsts of Greenup County

The first house built in Greenupsburg was built by Lewis Wilcoxen on lower Water Street near the mouth of Little Sandy River.

The first session of court met in the home of Andrew Hood, February 20, 1804.

The first courthouse was a frame building erected by Benjamin Locke on the public square in 1806. It was built of white pine and cost $900.

The first jail, a log building, was located near where the Methodist church now stands, and was built in 1806.

The first sheriff was Josiah Davidson, in 1804.

The first county clerks were Isaac Hockaday, in 1804, and John Hockaday, in 1805.

The first circuit judge was John Colvin, in 1805.

The first commonwealth attorney was James Clark.

The first case in court was Christopher Stump versus Aaron Littlejohn.

The first tax commissioner was James Howe.

The first schoolteacher was Silas Wooten.

The first doctor was Henry Green.

The first ferryman was Reason Davis, who was a hatter.

The first tavern keeper was Oba Timberlake.

The first merchant was Benjamin Chinn.

The Greenup Academy was built in 1815.

The first postmaster was Joshua Bartlett, in 1811.

The first orchard was planted by Andrew Hood.

James McGuire built the first carpenter shop.

Robert Lindsay preached the first sermon in the town of Green-upsburg.

The first prisoner in the jail was a man named Byrman, who struck and killed William Webb.

The first marriage license was issued to John Walker and Rachel McCool. The couple was married by Jacob Kouns.

The first representative was Charles N. Lewis.

The first senator was Thompson Ward.

The first steamboat on the Ohio River was the *New Orleans*, in 1811.

A covered wooden bridge was built across the Little Sandy River near the mouth in the 1840's or early 1850's.

The present iron bridge across Little Sandy River was built in 1884.

The first electric-light system was installed in 1896 by James M. Sowards.

The first telephone system was installed in 1900 by a Flemings-burg company.

Land Grants

After the close of the Revolutionary War, Virginia gave land called grants to those who had served in the war. Many were in the newly settled land of Kentucky. The most important person to receive a grant in Greenup County was Patrick Henry, the famous orator. His land consisted of two hundred acres opposite the mouth of the Scioto River. Later he received a second grant of two hundred acres, which adjoined the first. So far as is known, Patrick Henry never came to view his land.

Records in Mason County show that three men, Edmund Taylor, John Harvey, and Charles M. Thurston, were granted ten thousand acres in Mason County, of which Greenup County, at that time, was a part. When Greenup County was formed this grant extended along Tygart Creek and the Ohio River. Part of this land was sold to Benjamin Cooke, of Virginia, who had married Nancy, daughter of Moses Fuqua, Sr., on October 12, 1812. Benjamin Cooke deeded to Thomas B. and Nancy Cooke King "land from the mouth of Tygart Creek up the Ohio River to the first gut."

Abraham Buford received a grant of five thousand acres in the eastern section of the county. This became the property of his son, Charles, who sold the land to the Mead, Powell and Chinn families.

Josiah Morton was a Revolutionary soldier. He served at the Battle of Guilford Courthouse and was at the Siege of Yorktown. He was given a large grant of land lying west of Tygart Creek, which extended west as far as Stoner Hill. The Morton family came to this grant about 1800. Josiah died in 1838 and is buried on the grant, not far from the original home.

Charles Womack received a grant of two thousand acres lying along the Little Sandy River. He was a bachelor and never came to his land. When he died he left his land to a nephew, Charles Womack of Virginia, who sold it to the William Womack family of Oldtown. Much of this land has been sold in small tracts.

William Lindsay Poage patented a large parcel of land in the eastern section of the county adjoining the Buford grant in 1826. Mr. Poage formed a company to build Bellefonte Furnace and later Amanda Furnace, both on the Poage patent. General Robert Pogue, who fought under General Wayne against the Indians, and had settled in Mason County, bought eight thousand acres on Tygart Creek. This land was left to his son, who sold a great deal of it in farm tracts.

John Young patented a "tract of land lying between the Big Sandy and the Little Sandy Rivers" at what is now Palmyra.

Peter Taylor patented a tract of land at Wurtland. This became the property of Hon. John McConnell in 1819. The town of Wurtland is built on this land.

George Mason of Caroline County, Virginia, received a Treasury Warrant in 1873, of 2,748 acres on Tygart Creek. Part of this land was sold to Henry C. Coleman by Mason. This section was known as Culpepper for many years.

Thomas Lloyd Gray had taken the Oath of Allegiance in Prince George County, Virginia, in 1779. He served in the Revolutionary Army and had received a warrant for two hundred acres of land on the Ohio River.

There were many smaller grants made to those who came to the new land. It is not known why some of the lands were patented, or why Treasury Warrants were issued to some of the early settlers instead of the usual grants. (This may have been that only native Virginians could receive grants from Virginia.)

Indians

Kentucky was never a permanent home for any tribe of Indians. It was a "happy hunting ground," the dense forests furnishing shelter for many kinds of animals, turkeys and other game birds. The many salt springs—salt licks—were frequented by both Indians and animals.

Indian tribes came in the late autumn, "Indian summer," to kill deer for food and to prepare the skins for their clothing and tents. They hunted the turkey as much for feathers for head-dresses as for food. Members of different tribes met here, and so many battles occurred between these that Kentucky became known as "The Dark and Bloody Ground." The Indians were on friendly terms with the white traders, exchanging their valuable furs for the gaudy trinkets of the traders, but resented the coming of the settlers.

So far as has been known there were no battles fought between the Indians and the white men within the border of the present county. Many different tribes came, as is shown by the relics found in widely separated areas and made of many kinds of flint.

Mound And Ancient Monuments,
Greenup Co. Ky.

Northern tribes followed the Great Warriors Path southward, passing through Central Ohio and crossing the Ohio River at the mouth of the Scioto. Two prongs of the Warriors Path crossed the Ohio River, the second one at Cabin Creek in Mason County. One of these was on the way to Upper Blue Lick Springs and the other to Lower Blue Licks.

A formation at Siloam points to a higher civilization than that possessed by the Indians, and is supposed to have been connected with other formations north of the Ohio River. This formation has been termed a temple mound. It has three walls around a central mound, each having an opening on a different side. A formation on the Biggs Farm has but one wall, enclosing a central mound. A plainly marked roadway on the south side suggests it may have been erected for a protection for traveling settlers against the Indians. Many relics have been found in the field around it, which has been known as the Fort Field by the family.

Marcius Willson's *American History of 1847* describes the earthworks at old Springville as follows: "On the south side of the Ohio opposite Alexandria is an extensive enclosure, nearly square, whose walls of earth are from fourteen to twenty feet in height. At the south west corner is a mound twenty feet high and covering about half an acre. East and west of this enclosure are walls of earth, nearly parallel, half a mile or more in length and about two rods apart. These walls are now not more than four to six feet in height." (This place was marked several years ago by a historical society, The Colonial Dames.)

II

Early Court Records

County Court

On THE twentieth day of February, 1804, a small group of men met at the home of Andrew Hood for the purpose of establishing a court of sessions for the new county.. Thomas Waring, Jesse Boone and Seriah Stratton were appointed justices of the court; John Nichols, Reuben Rucker, John Davis Poage, Charles N. Lewis, Moses Fuqua, Jr., John Chadwick, Jacob Lockwood, and George Hardwick were appointed justices of the peace; Josiah Davidson was appointed sheriff; James Howe commissioner of revenue, and Isaac Hockaday temporary clerk of the court. These appointments were made by Governor James Garrard.

On a motion made by Jesse Boone, three men, John Mackoy, Josiah Davidson and Andrew Wolf, were appointed "to view the best way for a road to be opened from the county line opposite the mouth of the Big Scioto River to the mouth of the Big Sandy River."

James Clark and Thomas Daugherty qualified as attorneys-at-law, with James Clark being appointed commonwealth attorney.

The first juries were composed of Robert Poage, Robert Davidson, William Lowery, John Davis Poage, David Ellington, Benjamin Ulen. Thomas Hood, Absalom Burton, Jesse Griffith, James Lowery, James Norton, James McGinness, James Warnick, John Howe, John Terrill, Andrew Hood and William Dupuy.

County Court Justices

In 1804, the governor of Kentucky appointed eight justices. These were Reuben Rucker, John Nichols, John Davis Poage, Charles N. Lewis, Moses Fuqua, Jr., John Chadwick, George Hardwick and Jacob Lockwood. Succeeding judges, from 1804 to 1850, were:

Thomas Waring	John Hollingsworth
Jesse Boone	Samuel Bartley
Seriah Stratton	Basil Waring
John Poage	Jehu Rice
Benjamin Chinn	George Naylor Davis
Jonathan Morton	Samuel Gammon
Jacob Ham	Jesse Corum
Robert Grayson	Robert J. Harrison
Robert Henderson	John Brown
Richard Wheatley	William Kouns
David Brown	William Hampton
James VanBibber	Jesse Poynter
John R. Chitwood	Clement H. Waring
James Ward, Jr.	Abraham Crooks
Thomas B. King	Robert Laughlin
Martin Smith	Christian Spangler
Nimrod Canterbury	James Stewart
William Lowry	Benjamin F. King
Levi Shortridge	James Bryan
John C. Kouns	William A. Womack

Circuit Court

On May 6, 1806, circuit court was established, with the Hon. John Colvin, circuit judge; Thomas Waring and Jesse Boone, assistant judges; John Hockaday, clerk; Thomas Grayson, commonwealth attorney; Thomas Daugherty, David Trimble, Robert Grayson, James Clark and William Roper, attorneys-at-law.

On July 7, 1806, a court record "ordered that Jacob Kouns, Moses Fuqua and Charles N. Lewis let out and superintended the building of a courthouse in the Public Square." A copy of the description of the proposed building, made by Robert Robb, is contained in *A History of Greenup County.* This was built of logs and was in use until the completion of the brick building in 1816. The latter was in use until damaged by the 1937 flood, when it was razed and the present one built on the site.

The first jail stood near the site of the present Methodist Church.

In 1811 Jesse Boone was allowed £3.8 for building a jail on the south side of the Public Square. The Clerk's Office was built about the same time. Bricks for each of the three buildings were burned on the Alexander Rankins farm west of the town. The first jailers were John Bartley, Joshua Bartley, Oba Timberlake and Andrew Biggs. In the Circuit Clerk's Office are two letters written by Henry Clay in 1812 and 1819. A letter and a receipt from Abraham Lincoln is dated 1831. A record of 1815 ordered that the sheriff pay Benjamin Locke and Amos Kimball $258 for finishing the courthouse. The building came into use in 1816. A record of 1817, which may have been the first of the kind in the county, was a paper by the court permitting the emancipation of Jack, not infirm nor aged, by the owner George N. Davis.

In 1851, at the December term of circuit court, it was ordered that Alexander Rankins be allowed the sum of $10 for ferrying the grand jury and militiamen for the past year. The Little Sandy Bridge was built soon after this time.

County Judges

In 1850, judges took the place of justices, they being:

James Bryan	1850	J. Watt Womack	1912
John Poage	1854	Lewis Nicholls	1916
John Seaton	1858	Dow Quillen	1922
J. D. McCoy	1862	William Wheatley	1930
Wm. J. Worthington	1866	J. R. Shepherd	1934
A. L. Reid	1870	Jacob Fisher	1938
Lewis Nicholls	1884	G. W. Burchett	1942
J. W. Kouns	1892	Earl McKenzie	1945
Joseph Bennett	1898	William Adkins	1949
William T. Cole	1900	Delbert McKenzie	1953
W. J. A. Rardin	1908	Arthur Sparks	1957
	Beekham Mongomery	1961	

Circuit Judges

The list of circuit judges was furnished by Judge James R. Sowards:

Thomas Waring	1804	Adam Beatty	1823
Jesse Boone		William Roper	1824
Seriah Stratton		Walker Reed	1833
John Coburn	1805	Silas Robbins (special)	1835
Thomas Waring		James W. Moore	1851
Jesse Boone		Elijah C. Phister	1856
William McClung	1811	L. W. Andrews	1964
Thomas Waring		R. H. Stanton	1868
Jesse Boone		George Morgan Thomas	1874
Adam Beatty	1815	William H. Wadsworth	
W. T. Barry	1816	(special)	1876
Benjamin Miller	1818	Alfred E. Cole	1882
Eli Shortridge	1819	Stephen G. Kinner	1906
Silas Robbins	1822	William C. Halbert	1912
James P. Harbison	1893	Harvey Parker	1931
	James R. Sowards	1946	

Circuit Clerks

In 1870, a law was passed separating county and circuit clerks. The circuit clerks were as follows:

Charles Davidson	1870-1912	John Setser	1928-1934
Charles B. Bennett	1912-1916	William Coldiron	1934-1940
James D. Atkinson	1916-1922	Maynard Bush	1940-1949
Kelly Spears	1922-1928	Don Crum	1949-

County Clerks

Isaac Hockaday	1803-1804	Alva Cochran	1916-1922
John Hockaday	1804-1836	Joseph B. Bates	1922-1938
William Corum	1836-1876	John Millis	1938-1950
George Corum	1876-1908	J. L. O'Bryan	1950-1962
Stephen Howland	1908-1916	Leslie H. Moore	1962-
John Pritchard	1916-1916		

Members of the Legislature from Greenup County

SENATORS

Thompson Ward	1820-1826	Henry M. Rust	1857-1861
John M. McConnell	1826-1830	Wm. J. Worthington	1865-1869
William Conner	1830-1834	George T. Halbert	1878-1882
William G. Carter	1834-1838	J. B. Hannah	1890-1894
William Conner	1842-1846	Thomas H. Poynter	1905-1909
John C. Kouns	1850-1857	J. Howard Williams	1914-1918
	Dr. Henry T. Morris	1918-1926	

Henry M. Rust enlisted in the Army in 1861, was wounded November 7, 1861, in the Battle of Ivy Mountain, and died November 7. His body was sent to Greenup County for burial.

REPRESENTATIVES

Charles N. Lewis	1813-1815	Marcus L. Williams	1850-1851
Thompson Ward	1815-1818-1830	William C. Grier	1851-1853
Francis H. Gaines	1816-1820	Christopher C. Chinn	1853-1855
Thomas T. G. Waring	1819-1821	Joseph Patton	1857-1859
John M. McConnell	1822-1825	William C. Ireland	1859-1863
William Conner	1825-1827-1847	Edward F. Dulin	1863-1865
John C. Kouns	1828-1831	John D. Russell	1865-1869
Samuel Seaton	1831-1833-1845	James C. Waring	1869-1873
John C. Hollingsworth	1823-1835	Dr. Samuel Ellis	1873-1875
David Trimble	1836-1840	Marshall Baker	1875-1877
Basil Waring	1840-1841	W. H. H. Callihan	1877-1879
Robinson M. Biggs	1841-1842	George W. Thompson	1879-1880
Joseph D. Collins	1842-1843	B. F. Warnock	1880-1882
Jesse Corum	1844-1846	John T. King	1882-1884
Jefferson Evans	1846-1848	Wm. J. Worthington	1884-1886
James W. Davis	1848-1849	W. J. A. Rardin	1886-1890
Richard Jones	1849-1855-1857	J. Watt Womack	1890-1892

B. F. Bennett	1892-1896	J. G. Swearingen	1926-1930
D. J. McCoy	1896-1898	Russell O. Miller	1930-1932
R. C. Myers	1898-1900	Earl R. Stephens	1932-1934
Benj. F. Meadows	1900-1902	Mary Breckinridge	1934-1936
Wm. J. Worthington	1902-1906	C. C. Byrne	1936-1940
C. W. G. Hannah	1906-1910	Henry Stewart	1940-1942
J. Howard Williams	1910-1914	E. R. Hilton	1946-1956
James A. Scott	1914-1916	R. C. Holbrooks	1944-1946
A. S. Cooper	1916-1920	E. R. Hilton	1946-1950
C. C. Oney	1920-1924	James Lyons	1957-1962
Henry J. Kegley	1924-1926	L. St. Nicholls	1962-

These lists were furnished by Mr. Frank K. Kavanaugh of Frankfort, Kentucky.

Sheriffs

William Adkins compiled a list of high sheriffs and deputies during his term of office 1946-1949. The following is a list of the high sheriffs. A complete list of sheriffs and their deputies is contained in *A History of Greenup County*.

Joseph Davidson	1803-1805	Robert McCallister	1865-1868
Reuben Rucker	1806-1809	John Brooks	1869-1870
Charles Lewis	1810-1811	John D. Russell	1871-1874
Moses Fuqua, Jr.	1812-1813	Geo. N. Biggs (appointed)	1874
Jacob Kouns	1814-1815	B. F. Warnock	1875-1878
Reuben Canterbury	1816-1817	J. W. Kouns	1879-1882
Francis Waring	1818-1819	J. Watt Womack	1883-1886
John Poage	1820-1822	W. B. Taylor	1887-1890
Ben Chinn	1823-1824	John T. Womack	1891-1892
Robert Henderson	1825-1826	Matthew Warnock	1893-1894
James Ward	1827-1828	James B. Morton	1895-1897
Thomas B. King	1828-1829	John W. Collins	1898-1901
Thomas T. G. Waring	1830-1831	Samuel Bailey	1902-1905
John Culver	1832-1833	Patrick Artis	1906-1909
Thomas H. Poage	1834-1835	Taylor Lawson	1910-1913
John C. Kouns	1836-1837	W. M. Arthurs	1914-1917
James Bartley	1838-1839	J. Harve Elam	1918-1921
Geo. N. Davis	1840-1841	Vernon Callihan	1922-1925
Sam'l W. Gammon	1842-1843	Edward Tinsley	1926-1929
Clement H. Waring	1844-1845	George Crisp	1930-1933
Basil Waring	1846-1847	Jacob Fisher	1934-1937
Samuel Ratcliff	1848-1849	G. W. Burchett	1938-1941
John Brown	1850	Earl McKenzie	1942-1945
Roger Waring	1851	William Adkins	1946-1949
Marshall Baker	1852-1855	Delbert McKenzie	1950-1953
Geo. N. Darlington	1856-1860	Arthur Sparks	1954-1957
James Morton	1861	Beckham Montgomery	1957-1960
Adolphus Reid	1862-1864	Edward Wellman	1962-

NOTE: In 1850, John Brown was High Sheriff. In 1851, Roger Waring was High Sheriff. In 1852, Marshall Baker was High Sheriff. Allen Myers was probably jailer during these years.

Old News

A Little Journey into the Past History of Greenup County was made in the early 1900's by Ollan Bierley, a resident of Greenup. He wrote, "Tavern keeping at that time was a business that many would enter, once the permission of the court was granted. Records show that not every applicant for a license got by the careful judge and county attorney. It appears that fully a year's time was taken by the court officials in passing upon an applicant and often a license was not granted until the succeeding term of court and fully two thirds of them were refused. One's reputation had great bearing upon the Court, but politics, too, prevailed for some applicants got by the court easily while many continually failed its favors. One citizen, whose application had been refused many times, created quite a disturbance in the courtroom and drew a fine of $3 and costs." To the July, 1853, term of court came Abraham Willinok and Conrad Grote, and produced in court certificates duly authenticated, and declared their intentions of becoming citizens of the United States, and the necessary proof having been submitted, they were awarded the usual admission papers.

The following gentlemen served on the grand jury: James McMullen, foreman, Calvin Carnifax, John Howe, Joseph Davidson, Jesse Davidson, John Hartley, H. A. Poage, Edward Brooks, Daniel Iliff, Vincent Colvin, Acy Bellew, Elza Allison, William Jones, N. F. Thom, George Womack and Jabez Z. Coe. The judge was James Bryan. Until 1850 justices served the county and James Bryan became the first county judge.

March 29, 1857—The clerk was directed to bind out to Robert McCallister Ann Elizabeth Scott, a poor child born April 30, 1847, until she should arrive at 21. Kyle Scott, 13, was bound out to William Bevins until he was 21.

In the county election, August, 1858, William Corum was re-elected clerk. He appointed Alexander Smith his deputy for a new term. S. H. Walcott was elected surveyor, John C. Adams county judge, George E. Roe county attorney. Upon motion of the clerk, Alexander Smith, John Clark, John Seaton, H. C. Poage, A. C. Van Dyke and Lyndsay Dodge were appointed deputies. Allen Myers was re-elected jailer.

October 4, 1858—Be it remembered that on this day personally appeared in court William S. Kouns, Allen Myers, Lewis D. Ross, and John M. Powell, and upon their solemn oath declared that they were well acquainted with Henry Reimlinger, late of

Greenup County, deceased, and that the said Henry Reimlinger came to his death by drowning in the Ohio River, in Greenup County, December 16, 1858, leaving a widow named Joanna Reimlinger and a child named Ferdinand William surviving him and also a child by a former marriage, Henrietta Frederick Mayer, and that the deceased was buried on the day succeeding his death in the graveyard near the town of Greenupsburg.

January, 1859—Ella Ann Griffith, an infant orphan with no estate, was bound out to John Weeks as an apprentice to the trade of seamstress.[1]

Hangtown

The following account of the Brewer murder was given in 1950 to the author by Mrs. Albert Hales, a resident of Wolf Pen, Greenup County, and a granddaughter of John Collins. Parts of this were printed in *A History of Greenup County*. Greenupsburg got its name of Hangtown as a result of many public hangings which took place near the town. People came from far and near and made the hangings a sort of gala occasion. They came in their best bibs and tuckers.

The last public hanging took place in June, 1852. Hon. J. W. Moore was circuit judge, but, due to illness, Judge Thomas H. Hazelrigg was appointed to fill the vacancy, and presided at the trial. Court records show that Turner and Ruben Clark, John and Bill Hood and John Collins were charged with the murder of a man by the name of William Brewer and his wife over a line fence and lesser quarrels between Collins and Brewer. The murder occurred on East Fork of Little Sandy River. Records show that Collins was the ringleader and hired his companions to commit the actual murder by having them go to the Brewer home and create a disturbance in the chickenyard. Upon the appearance of Brewer he was beaten to death with a club. When his wife appeared at the sound of the commotion, she was killed also, as records show.

It required three days to conduct the trial. The jury, W. R. Smith, Abram Meadows, Evan Jackson, Moses Mackoy, Thomas McNeal, Timothy Clary, John T. Lawson, David Smith, James Alley, A. J. Enslow, A. G. Womack and John Sloan, returned verdicts of death in the cases of John Collins, Turner and Ruben Clark, while John and Bill Hood were given life sentences. Of the

[1] NOTE: Other news of the 1850's is contained in *A History of Greenup County*, of 1951-1952.

three receiving the death penalty, two actually paid it on the scaffold, Collins hung himself in the jail prior to the day of execution. John and Bill Hood were later released from prison to serve as soldiers in the Civil War. One of these met his death by drowning while attempting to ford the Cumberland River, while the other lived to an advanced age.

A description of the hanging was furnished by a Greenupsburg man, Zachariah Richards, a Civil War veteran, whose father was also a guard on the occasion. "On the day of the execution, Greenupsburg was filled to overflowing, people coming for miles on horseback, mules, in wagons and on foot. A drum and fife corps was on hand to play the death march. The spot on which the scaffold was erected was at the west end of Main Street, on the bank of Little Sandy. On the opposite bank stood an old deserted water mill, which formed a vantage point for many of the curious. The high bank on the upper side also furnished a favorable site for onlookers. As the slowly driven ox-cart (they had to use oxen on account of the noise and commotion caused by the music and huge crowd, making horses hard to manage) bearing the coffins of the condemned, and the prisoners seated thereon, worked its way up to and under the scaffold, where the black caps were placed in position, the fife and drum corps played the death march. At a given signal the noose was adjusted, the ox-cart moved on and the bodies dangled in the air."

There were women as well as men in attendance by the hundreds. They were dressed in the latest fashion. Many women were dressed in the costly attire of that time, consisting of dress skirts that took many yards to make, with goods retailing at $3 a yard, their feet encased in fine calf shoes. On parted and puff-combed hair rested hats with extreme high crowns and very narrow brims. Men were present with great mustaches, in costly array of bleached-muslin pleated shirts, bluejean trousers and nail-keg hats.

The Courthouse Bell

On July 24, 1953, the following article appeared in the *Greenup News:* "Sessions of Court are to be heralded by the ringing of the courthouse bell. When the new building was erected after the old courthouse was razed when badly damaged by the flood of 1937, the bell remained in the courtyard until the above date when the Fiscal Court had it placed in the tower of the new courthouse." William Adkins was the county judge at that time.

We have never been able to learn when and where the first bell was purchased for the courthouse that was built in 1811-1816 and razed in 1937-1938. In January, 1859, the presiding judge, John C. Adams, went to Pittsburgh as special commissioner, to purchase the bell which has been in use since. The old bell was exchanged "with much additional currency for the new one."

III

Outstanding Citizens

THOMAS H. PAYNTER was born in Lewis County. He studied law and, about 1875, came to Greenup, where he practiced his profession with great success. He entered politics, and in 1905 he was elected state senator and served one term, then was elected to the United States Senate. Although a Democrat, he was popular with the people of other parties. The Paynter family moved to Washington, where they resided for many years. When Mr. Paynter was appointed a federal judge, the family moved to Frankfort, Kentucky.

Mr. Paynter married Elizabeth, daughter of Joseph and Sarah Kouns Pollock, May 21, 1879. They were the parents of two children, Winifred, who married Morton K. Yonts of Louisville, and Pollock, now of Frankfort, both of whom were born in Greenup. Mr. and Mrs. Paynter are buried in the Frankfort Cemetery.

Joseph Bentley Bennett was born at Bennett's Mill in Greenup County. When he was a young man the family moved to Greenup. He studied law and began his practice in the county, being associated with his father, Benjamin F. Bennett. He was a Republican in politics and was elected county judge, county attorney, and served eight years in Congress. When his term as congressman expired the family returned to Greenup, where he resumed the practice of law.

Mr. Bennett married Anna, daughter of C. W. Mytinger of Greenup, August 30, 1883, and they were the parents of nine children: Arthur, who married Esther Morton of Greenup, and who made their home in Washington, D.C.; Charles Bentley, who married Lucille Wilson and lived in Greenup, Frances, Katharine, Emmabelle, Julia, Mary, Sallie and Joseph. The latter ones married and made their homes elsewhere.

William Jackson Worthington was born in Westmoreland County, Pennsylvania, in 1832. The family moved to Ohio and

[35]

later to Greenup County. He was captain of Company B of the Twenty-second Kentucky Volunteer Infantry in the Civil War, was commissioned a major and later a lieutenant-colonel. After the war he returned to Greenup County and became interested in Raccoon Furnace, where the family lived until 1882 when he bought the William Corum property near Riverton. He studied law and practiced in Greenup County. He was a Republican and served as county judge, representative, and state senator. In 1895 he was elected lieutenant-governor of Kentucky.

Colonel Worthington was married twice and had five children by his first wife. Late in life he married Lucy York, of Hunnewell, and they were the parents of two daughters, Mrs. Patterson Williams of Russell, and Mrs. James Collins of Greenup.

Mr. Bates married Virginia, daughter of Larkin Monroe and Anna Laura Rice of Wurtland. They are the parents of Joseph R. and Rebecca, wife of Shannon Vinson. The three families live at Riverton.

Citizens of Greenup

We show a picture taken in 1884 on the river grade. The former courthouse stands in the rear of the clerk's office and on the corners are the law offices of Jeremiah Davidson and Judge William Sands. The business buildings on Harrison Street may also be seen.

When this picture was made Lewis E. Nicholls was county judge, J. Watt Womack was sheriff, George A. Corum was county clerk, which office he had held for forty years, and Charles Davidson was the first circuit clerk. These officials are included in the picture, and others are Thomas Paynter, Edward Dulin, F. B. Trussell, Jeremiah Davidson, W. J. A. Rardin, B. F. Bennett, Bud Roe, Butler Taylor, James Stark, John Womack, Scott Clifton, Will McKee, Fred Ault, Cal Callon, Zeke Coffee, Thomas Jacobs, Silas Greenslate. (Between pages 96-97.)

N.B.: This picture first appeared in the *Russell Times* Anniversary Edition of 1942 and used in this *Supplementary Edition of A History of Greenup County* by permission of Editor E. O. Mitterdorf.

Jesse Stuart Day

Jesse Stuart Day, October 15, 1955, sponsored by the Lions Club, was observed at Greenup to honor Jesse Stuart, poet, essayist, novelist and lecturer. This was the largest gathering ever seen in the town and, to quote an old poem, "There was such a crowd, there was scarce room to stand."

While lecturing at Murray State College Auditorium, Murray, Kentucky, Mr. Stuart collapsed, stricken with a heart attack, having overtaxed his strength too often. For four months he was a convalescent. His friends, neighbors and readers were deeply concerned over his condition. To show this, and their appreciation for his literary achievements, they decided to place a memorial in his honor while he was living. All were instrumental in bringing this to a reality.

The following program was arranged for "the day," with the ceremonies held on the courthouse lawn:

> Parade of bands and floats, beginning at the high school at Riverton and ending at the courthouse square.
> National Anthem and raising of the flag.
> Invocation—The Rev. Guy Coffman, Pastor of the Methodist Church.
> Address of Welcome—Master of Ceremonies, Judge James R. Sowards.
> Address—Dr. Robert L. Kincaid, President of Lincoln Memorial University, Harrogate, Tennessee.
> Address—Dr. Herman L. Donovan, President of University of Kentucky, Lexington, Kentucky.
> Response—Jesse Stuart.
> Unveiling of Memorial—Jessica Jane Stuart.

The bands of Greenup, Raceland, and McKell Schools participated in the colorful parade. The floats depicted various books written by Mr. Stuart. These were: *Man with a Bull-Tongue Plow, Taps for Private Tussie, Hie to the Hunters, The Thread That Runs So True, The Good Spirit of Laurel Ridge,* and others.

The book of poems, *Man with a Bull-Tongue Plow,* published in 1934, was Mr. Stuart's first writing to win fame for him, and brought to him the Guggenheim Fellowship and a trip to Europe. It has been recognized as a true classic and one of the one hundred best books in America. His hilarious *Taps for Private Tussie* has passed the million mark in sales. The book of poems, *Kentucky Is My Land* has won acclaim. *The Thread That Runs So True* is the story of Mr. Stuart's earlier experiences as a teacher and it has been held up as one of the great books on practical education.

Mr. Stuart is one of America's best-known authors—with eighteen books and more than five hundred published short stories bearing his name. He has been a nationally known lecturer, with some two thousand speeches before an estimated two million people from east to west coasts, and he has received honorary doctorates from four different colleges.

Doctor Meadows Day

June 13, 1955, was Doctor Meadows Day at Fullerton and South Shore, where the many friends of Dr. Matthew Warnock Meadows met to honor the eighty-seven-year-old physician who had served the western area of the county for over fifty years. The "day" began at 1 P.M. with open house at the Harrison Fullerton Masonic Lodge, where the doctor was greeted by a large number of his friends. Later, the long procession of cars moved to McKell High School, where a banquet was held in the evening.

The speaker for the evening was Rev. Omar Miller of the Russell Christian Church, who was one of the five thousand babies that first saw the light of day through the ministrations of Dr. Meadows. There were many others of these present.

Dr. Meadows was born in Tygart in 1868. He is a son of Benjamin F. and America Warnock Meadows. He married Miss Lula Holbrook of Tygart and, in 1904, settled at Fullerton to practice his profession. They are the parents of three sons, Frank, Herman and Russell. Frank married Miss Mariana Merrill and resides in Greenup. He has a son, William Matthew. Herman and Russell are residents of Morehead, the former having married Miss Maxine Caudill of that town.

Biographies

In 1929 *A History of Kentucky*, containing the names of prominent citizens of the state, was written. A copy of this is in the Young Men's Christian Association Library at Russell, Kentucky. The Greenup citizens mentioned therein are Joseph Bentley Bennett, William Alexander Biggs, Joseph Bengal Bates, Charles Bentley Bennett, William Throop Cole, George Alexander Corum, George Darby, John Taylor Lawson, Dr. Henry Thomas Morris, Robert Joseph Nickel, Thomas Earl Nickel, John Edward Pollock, James Watt Womack, Robert E. Lee Wilson, William Milton Stevens, and Daniel J. Taft.

The names of Russell citizens contained in the history are William Salyers Butler, James Carman, Jacob Fisher, Vernon R. Jones, Robert Taylor Parsons, Archie Stark Morgan, John W. Stephens, Henry Armistead Williams, Patrick Anderson Williams, and Dr. Charles Edward Whitt.

Lawyers (1804-1956)

Thomas Grayson	B. F. Bennett
James Clark	William J. Sands
Thomas Dougherty	George Halbert
David Trimble	Thomas H. Paynter
William Roper	Benjamin E. Roe
Robert G. Grayson	Joseph B. Bennett
Thompson Ward	William T. Cole
John McConnell	Thomas Nickell
William Conner	James D. Atkinson
John C. Hollingsworth	Lovell Liles
William Ireland	C. H. Bruce
Edward Dulin	John Coldiron
F. B. Trussell	Frank Warnock
William Worthington	James Lyon
George Roe	Joseph B. Bates
Jeremiah Davidson	Lewis Nicholls

Physicians (1804-1956)

Henry Green	Greenupsburg
James Van Bibber	Greenupsburg
Alfred Spalding	Greenupsburg
Samuel Ellis	Greenupsburg
Alfred DeBard	Greenupsburg
James Gibson	Laurel Furnace
David C. Munn	Limeville
C. M. Brammer	Wurtland
James M. Moore	Tygart Valley
Charles Secrest	Lynn
Benjamin F. Bennett	Tygart Valley
Alonzo Carnahan	Oldtown
Romulus C. Biggs	Smith Branch
John T. Sellards	Greenup
Abram Sellards	Greenup
A. S. Brady	Greenup
M. S. Leslie	Greenup
Henry T. Morris	Greenup
Ellis Raike	Lynn
Matthew W. Meadows	Fullerton
A. J. Bryson	Fullerton
Ellis Nichols	Fullerton
R. M. Biggs	Frost
H. H. Holbrook	Greenup

Edward Fitch ....Russell
James Rathbone ....Russell
William Morris ....Fullerton
O. P. Clark ....Russell
C. S. Vidt ....Russell
C. B. Johnson ....Russell
C. A. Thompson ....South Shore
W. A. Riddle ....South Shore
Charles Conley ....Greenup

A List of Greenup County Citizens of 1811

Alexander, John
Allison, John
Anglin, Gabriel
Anglin, John
Bacon, Benedict
Bainfield, Thomas
Ball, James
Ball, Robert
Bar, Henry
Barklow, Ruth
Barley, Wiatt
Barnes, Robert
Bartley, John
Bartley, Joshua
Baset, Amos
Bean, Stephen
Bell, Thompson
Benough, George
Biggs, Douglas
Blackburn, William
Blake, Kenneth
Blankenship
Boone, Jesse
Boone, Nathan
Bradshaw, George
Bradshaw, William
Bragg, Armstead
Barklow, Ruth
Broomfield, Skinner
Brown, Davis
Brown, John
Brown, Nelson
Brubaker, Abraham
Bruce, John
Bruce, William
Bryan, John
Bryan, Zephaniah
Bryson, William
Buckhannon, William
Buckles, Robert
Burbridge, Robert
Cain, John
Cam, Jacob

Cam, Job
Cam, Thomas
Campbell, Jesse
Campbell, Johnson
Cannon, John
Canterbury, Benjamin
Canterbury, John
Canterbury, Nimrod
Canterbury, Reuben
Carter, George
Carter, Hebe
Cartwright, Thomas
Cathwell, Robert
Catlett, Alex
Catlett, Alex, Jr.
Catlett, Horatio
Catlett, Elisha
Chadwick, John
Chaffin. Christopher
Chaffin, Nancy
Chapman, Reuben
Chinn, Benjamin
Chitwood, John R.
Clark, John
Clark, John, Jr.
Cob, John
Cohlin, Gideon
Colvin, John
Colvin, Samuel
Cornelius, Austin
Craig, William
Crank, Jacob
Crank, John
Crank, Joseph
Craycraft, Charles
Creekpaun, Michell
Culp, Conlas
Culp, Tilman
Curren, Joseph
Curry, Henry
Cummings, Henry
Davis, George N.
Davis, Rezin

Davis, Samuel
Davisson, Josiah
Deering, Anthony
Deering, Richard
Demint, Samuel
Downs, John
Drury, Salson (Lawson)
Duncan, Alexander
Duncan, Charles
Dummit, William
Dupuy, William
Durbin, Amos
Easom, Edward
Edwards, John
Ellington, John
Ellington, Pleasant
Evans, William
Everman, Jacob
Everman, John
Farmer, Jeremiah
Farmer, Joshua
Flaugher, Christian
Foster, Job
Friend, Andrew
Friend, Jacob
Friend, Jonas
Fuqua, David
Fuqua, Mary
Fuqua, Moses
Fuqua, Samuel
Fuqua, William
Gaine, Francis H.
Gammon, Richard
Garrett, Ignatius
Garden, Joseph
Gholson, William
Gibson, James
Gilkey, Edward
Goble, Abram
Goble, Daniel
Goble, Ephraim
Gorman, William
Grayson, Alfred

Grayson, George
Grayson, Robert
Greene, Robert H.
Greenslate, John
Hamm, Jacob
Hannah, Gabriel
Hannah, Robert
Hatch, Edward
Hatton, William
Hatton, Elijah
Hardwick, George
Hargus, John
Hedges, Solomon
Henderson, Robert
Henderson, Robert, Jr.
Hensley, George
Hitchcock, Caleb
Holland, Wright
Hockaday, John
Hood, Andrew
Hood, Thomas
Horseley, Taylor
Howe, James
Howe, John
Howe, Joseph
Huffman, Jacob
Huson, James
Jackson, Charles
Johnson, Levi
Jones, Peter
Jordan, William
Kibbee, Amos
Kibbee, Moses
Kilgour, David
Kiser, Jacob
Kite, James
Knap, Joshua
Kouns, Jacob
Kouns, John
Lacy, John
Lawson, Thomas
Lewis, Charles
Littlejohn, John
Littlejohn, Valentine
Lockwood, Jacob
Lowry, James
Lowry, John
Lowry, Melvin
Lowry, William
Lyons, Hezekiah
Mayhew, Ezra
Mayhew, Elijah
Mackoy, John
Madden, Nathan
McAlester, James
McCallister, James
McCallister, Luke

McGlone, Owen
McGlone, Andrew
McGuire, James
McGuire, John
McLaughlin, William
Meadow, James
Meek, Samuel
Meek, James
Miller, John
Miller, William
Morton, Jonathan
Morton, Josiah
Nicholls, Cassandra W.
Nicholls, John
Norman, Joseph
Norton, James
Osborne, William
Oscar, James
Parker, David
Parker, Elias
Parker, Robert
Parry, Daniel
Pettit, Matthew
Pettit, Samuel
Pickett, Younger
Pogue, Allen
Pogue, James
Pogue, Mary
Pogue, John
Porter, Jacob
Powell, Joseph
Price, Edmund
Price, Mordacai
Price, Sampson
Radcliffe, Daniel
Reason, Lewis
Rice, James
Richards, Thomas
Riddle, John
Roberts, Jesse
Robertson, Winslow
Rucker, Ambrose
Rucker, Ephraim
Rucker, Reuben
Scott, David
Scott, James
Scott, John
Scott, Thomas
Shelton, Joseph
Shields, John
Short, Aaron
Shortridge, Levi
Shortridge, Margaret
Skidmore, Joseph
Skidmore, Polly
Skidmore, Samuel
Slawter, Samuel

Smith, Martin
Smith, Robert
Smith, Randall
Smith, Samuel
Smith, Thomas
Solliday, Samuel
Sperry, James
Sperry, Samuel
Spriggs, Samuel
Starr, Koonrad
Stephenson, Richard
Stewart, Charles
Stewart, Matthew
Storey, John
Stratton, Seriah
Stratton, Jeremiah
Stump, Christopher
Terry, Thomas
Terry, William
Thompson, Andy
Thompson, James
Thompson, Samuel
Thompson, Waddy
Throckmorton, Joseph
Throckmorton, William
Timberlake, Oba
Tolbert, Thomas
Tyree, William
Ulen, Benjamin
Van Bibber, Jacob
Van Bibber, James
Van Bibber, Peter
Vice, Enoch
Virgin, Rezin
Virgin, Thomas
Ward, James
Ward, John
Ward, Thomas
Waring, Clement H.
Waring, Francis
Waring, James
Waring, Thomas
Waring, Thomas Truman
  Greenfield
Warnock, James
Warnock, Johnson
Warnock, Samuel
Warnock, William
Wells, John
Wheatly, Richard
White, David
White, William
White, Solomon
Wilcox, Lewis
Williams, Eli
Willit, Joseph
Wilson, Alexander

[41]

Wilson, Thomas	Womack, Archer	1813
Woods, Andrew	Young, Fountain	
Woolford, John	Young, John	Biggs, Andrew
Wooten, Charles	Zane, Andrew	King, Thomas B.
Wooten, Silas	Zane, Philip	

Negroes

The first Negroes were brought to Greenup County by their Virginia masters to clear land for farming. Those who brought the largest numbers were Martin Smith, who came with "fifty Negro slaves and settled above Greenup about 1800," and Charles Howland, who "brought many slaves with him" when he settled on Brushy Creek in Tygart. James Gilruth wrote, "Lewis Wilcoxen had slaves to clear the land of oak, beech and poplar trees" where he built the first house on the present site of Greenup.

Those pioneer Negroes were well-mannered and continued so after the Emancipation Proclamation made them free. There have always been the kindest feelings between the descendants of the two races. Negro families from south and west of the town settled on Perry Street, while those from farms east settled at Riverton, which due to the building of the Eastern Kentucky Railroad was a busy place. Farmers kept only those Negroes that were necessary for the work on the farm. Several of the families remained at Wurtland, where their descendants still own homes. As there seems to be no Smith name among these, it is possible it became absorbed into the Kouns name because of a marriage between the two families when Major John C. Kouns, a son of the pioneer family of Jacob Kouns that came from Pennsylvania in 1795, married Elizabeth, a daughter of Martin Smith. The Kouns family was responsible for the building of the "Fifteenth Amendment" as a home for Negroes after the Civil War. The Rawlins (Rollins) and Ulen Negroes remained on the original land of their white owners at Wurtland. Ben Ulen died on Ulens Branch at Wurtland not many years ago and was said to be over one hundred years old.

Negro children were taught in the homes of the owners until 1870, when a frame church and school combined was built beyond Perry Street. The first schools here were taught by Belle and Sadie McMullen, whose family lived near. The earliest Negro teacher was Fannie Carter. When later a brick school was built in East Greenup, local teachers were hired. Among these have been Jennie Ward, Laura King, Mattie Ward and Mary Louise King. In 1956, pupils were enrolled in the Greenup High School with kindliest feelings between white and colored.

[42]

Negroes who served in the Civil War were Harvey McConnell Jack and James Crump, Aaron Stratton, James Winn, Jack Kibby and William Rollins—the latter being buried in the Arlington Cemetery at Washington, D.C. Those who have served in world wars are Stanley and Edward McConnell, Robert and James Crump, Jack and Sam Ailster, Aubrey Rollins, Lewis Troxler, Ambrose Cosby and Herbert Jackson.

IV

U.S. Mail

IN THE early days of the county, mail was carried on horseback. One of these carriers was William Biggs (1800-1897) who, when a lad in his teens, carried the mail on horseback from the Big Sandy River to the Mason County line. When brought to Greenupsburg it was handled by a merchant whose store was probably on Harrison Street in one of several small buildings that stood between the Kouns House yard and the Dr. William Kouns Drug Store. When boats began to ply the river they carried the mail to points along it. When the Eastern Kentucky Railroad was built the train carried the mail of the southeastern section of the county. When the Chesapeake and Ohio Railroad was completed it took over much of the carrying of the mail of this section.

Forest Holdercamper of Washington, D.C., furnished the following concerning Greenup County: According to the record of the Post Office Department in Washington from 1789 to 1934, now in the National Archives, a post office was established in Greenupsburg (now Greenup) shortly before July 1, 1811. Names of postmasters and dates of their appointments were:

Joshua Bartlett—July 1, 1811	Wm. M. Stevens—Dec. 26, 1882
Samuel L. Crawford—April 1, 1813	Benj. F. Brown—July 16, 1885
Jesse B. Boone—March 21, 1814	Leonidas Callon—Aug. 21, 1888
Alphonso Boone—July 11, 1814	Wm. M. Stevens—April 2, 1889
Joseph Gardner—May 20, 1816	Herbert Reid—March 24, 1893
Henry E. Green—May 11, 1818	Thomas Myers—May 26, 1897
William W. Bunnel—Aug. 22, 1828	Charles Taylor—July 24, 1905
Charles M. Wilson—Dec. 11, 1833	Thomas Myers—Dec. 13, 1905
C. L. Raison—July 8, 1844	Charles Taylor—July 3, 1909
Joseph Pollock—March 19, 1850	J. D. McCoy—Aug. 2, 1913
Benj. F. Brown—Aug. 29, 1859	Eunice D. Taylor—Aug. 30, 1916
Joseph Pollock—July 9, 1861	Wm. I. Myers—March 1, 1922
Benj. F. Brown—Sept. 25, 1866	Ernest Warnock—May 27, 1929
Francis C. Robb—March 6, 1867	Mrs. Maggie Warnock—Oct. 1, 1932
John Moran—July 8, 1872	Mrs. Rebecca Forsythe—April, 1934

Frank L. Coldiron

Greenup County Post Offices

(Furnished by Frank L. Coldiron, P.M.)

Recent post offices discontinued were:

Wurtland—1959
Lynn—1959
Raceland—1958
Riverton—1958
Naples—1958
Warnock—1958
Tygarts Valley—1958
Siloam—1957

Graysbranch—1957
Tongs—1957
Brushart
Walsh
Hopewell—1956
Samaria—1956
Fullerton—1955

Three Rural Routes, Greenup, South Shore and Flatwoods Post Offices were established in 1957.

Greenup County Post Offices, March 1, 1960:

NAME	POSTMASTER
Russell	Elenor Millis
Flatwoods	Velma Lane
Greenup	Frank L. Coldiron
Argillite	Elizabeth Brewer
Oldtown	Dick Womack
Kehoe	Ewing Duncan
Maloneton	Mrs. Munn
South Shore	Mrs. Olive Brown
Load	Mrs. Wm. Darnell
South Portsmouth	Mrs. McElhaney
Letitia	Mr. Bentley
Worthington	Eugene Salmon
Lloyd	Minnie Herald
York	Mrs. Wm. Miller

More than one hundred and forty years have elapsed since the mail was carried through what are now the counties of Greenup, Lawrence, Carter and Boyd on horseback. This decade sees the mail on rural routes carried by automobiles or other motor vehicles.

Newspapers

The *Big Sandy News,* published at Catlettsburg in the early 1850's by E. C. Thornton and G. W. Smith, was probably the first newspaper in Greenup County. The first one in Greenupsburg was edited by George Creel, in the early 1870's, and later by Karl B. Grahn. This, the *Independent,* was edited by Carlisle Callon in 1879 and early 1880's.

[45]

H. B. Woodrow edited the *Greenup Gazette* in the 1880's. W. J. A. Rardin bought the press and fixtures and edited the paper for many years. In 1913 the press was badly damaged by the flood and the *Gazette* was discontinued. In 1892, the *Democrat* was edited by Samuel Callon and Robert Wilson in a building on Washington Street. Before this time the various printing offices had been located in the Masonic Building. The *Democrat* was later moved to the Myers Building on Front Street where it was edited by Walter Callon for five or six years, when it was discontinued.

About 1915, Seneca X. Swimm edited the *Republican* for one year, when Leo Thompson became editor for two years. In 1922 William I. Myers bought the press and edited the paper until 1934. The *Greenup News* and *Russell Times* are the current newspapers.

The Register of the Kentucky Historical Society of July, 1938, gives:

Newspapers in Ashland until 1859—
1856—*Ashland Republican*
1857—*Democratic Battery*
1860—*Sandy Valley Advocate*
Newspapers in Catlettsburg until 1853—
1852—*Big Sandy News*
1860—*Sandy Valley Advocate*
All of these newspapers were issued weekly.

Greenup County has two newspapers, *The News,* edited by Marvin Wilson of Greenup, and the *Russell Times,* edited by E. O. Mittendorf.

V

Early Business Builders

Greenupsburg, Greenup and Greenup County

THE EARLIEST business houses centered around the court square. These were small frame buildings and were known as shops instead of stores. In the 1850's and 1860's these began to be razed and were succeeded by brick buildings of such good material and honest workmanship that many of these are in excellent condition after more than one hundred years.

The three-story building on the corner of Main and Washington Streets was built about 1856, and during the three decades of 1870–1880–1890 Benjamin F. Brown operated a general store there. When Mr. Brown was appointed postmaster in 1866 the store housed the post office, and again in 1885 when he again was appointed postmaster. The two-story building next door was built some time later and was occupied by the James McMullan hardware store and tin shop. In 1889, when W. M. Stevens was appointed postmaster, this building housed the post office and again in 1934, when Mrs. Rebecca B. Forsythe became postmaster. It remained there twenty years. Some time in the 1860's Benjamin Pratt and Thomas Brooks erected a two-room, two-story building next to the McMullan store, one for dry goods and the other for groceries. Next to the Pratt and Brooks Building there stood until recent years a one-story frame building, the John Schmutz Tavern, which was the only building on the square to be razed and the present one built on the site. Across Elizabeth Street was the Stark Store Building, where the family operated a general store from the late 1850's until the early 1870's. Several small frame shops between Elizabeth and Water (Front) Streets were razed when David Trimble bought the four lots between Washington Street and Cedar Alley. During the 1870's other small buildings were erected on the site of those very early shops. These have been razed and a dwelling house stands on the corner of Elizabeth and Washington

Streets. A business house and storage building occupy the Trimble-Stark corner.

The clerk's office and two frame law offices occupied that part of Front from Washington to Harrison Streets. In the yard of the Kouns House on the corner of Front and Harrison Streets was a row of frame buildings, one of which housed the post office in very early times. Some of these were razed in the early 1880's when Nicholas Bergmeyer built the two-story building, later the Patton Hotel. One of these is still in use. The Dr. Will Kouns Drug Store, a frame structure, stands yet, used as a dwelling. The Joseph Pollock Bank next door now houses the fire department. On the corner is a brick building that was erected in the early 1870's by Amos Thornsbury, where he operated a general store before moving to Texas in the early 1880's. Across Elizabeth Street, where the Jehu Sydenstricker store burned in 1871 or 1872, is a frame two-story building that was occupied in the 1880's and later by a bakery and confectionery kept by John Bierly. The next-door building housed the Dickey-Hoop Shoe Store and the next the Dr. A. G. Sellards Drug Store. The Stevens-Pollock Hardware Store occupied the next building and, in the 1890's, it became Lawson and Biggs Store.

On the corner of Main and Harrison Streets a story-and-a-half red brick house was set back in a yard and fronted on Harrison Street. This was the home of the William Ireland family in the 1870's and much earlier. The Ireland family moved to Ashland, and this was the home of the John Mackoy family until about 1875, when they moved to Texas. The house was razed and A. L. Reid built a store on the corner which was operated by the family during the decades mentioned and was made into the present bank building. A grocery store that changed owners often occupied the present Kendall stores.

Across Main Street stands a very old one-story building, looking very much as it did in the decades. This was built after the Civil War by Joseph Pfaff for a residence and tailor shop. Children from up the street, down the street and from Front passed this corner (and still do) on their way out Harrison to a school that has always been in existence since the beginning in 1815.

On the corner of Main and Harrison Streets is the three-story brick building of the Masonic Temple, erected in the middle 1860's. The Dr. William Kouns Drug Store occupied the lower floor for many years. The Masonic Lodge occupies a room on Washington Street. Leslie's Drug Store occupies the Masonic

Building. When the Sydenstricker grocery burned in the early 1870's, Mr. Sydenstricker operated a store next door to the Masonic Building. This has been in use as a hardware store, Citizens Bank and post office. Two brick buildings stand on the site of the Jeremiah Davidson cottage of the 1870's. The Major Van Bibber home and office stand next, now owned and occupied by the Vernon Callihan family. A large two-story frame house stood on the corner of Main and Washington Streets. It was built by the Corum family for a tavern in the 1840's or 1850's. This became the home of the Jackson Jacobs family that moved to Texas in the late 1870's. The James Stark family occupied it in the 1880's and 1890's. James M. Sowards razed it and erected the present brick house and office where Mr. Sowards established the Farmers and Merchants Bank. This is the property of the Dr. Henry Morris family.

Taverns

Tavern keeping was a very necessary business in early settlements. Many taverns were in existence before licenses were issued. One of the first taverns in Greenupsburg was kept by Oba Timberlake at his home on Main Street between Harrison and Washington. He was the jailer from 1813 to 1816. At that time the jail was located on Main Street across from the Timberlake home.

The earliest records we find of licenses issued to tavern keepers are those to Joseph Gardner and to William M. Gholson in 1815, "who are permitted to keep tavern at their dwelling houses for one year after date." In 1816 Oba Timberlake was "permitted to keep tavern at his dwelling for one year after date." In 1818 Jacob Kouns was granted a tavern license and in 1820 licenses were granted to Richard Deering, Jesse England, Sam Seaton, Vincent Powell, Edward Damrell, John Green, John Miller, Sr., and John A. Jones. In 1822 James McGuire, ferryman, was issued license to keep tavern at his dwelling house on Water Street, and the same year John Kouns was granted a license.

Later tavern keepers were Samuel Powell, Thomas Garrett, Jesse Corum, Rezin Lyons, Jeremiah Davidson, and Samuel Osenton. On November 10, 1823, John Kouns advertised as follows: "John Kouns, with Edward Damrell and Thomas Poage, as bondsmen, obtains a license to keep tavern at his dwelling and obligates himself to constantly provide in his said tavern good wholesome food, cleanly lodging and such for travelers, stable provision for horse and etc."

For many years the Kouns House on the corner of Front and Harrison Streets was the principal stopping place for travelers. Robert Callihan kept the Andes House on Main Street in the 1870's and 1880's. This was the favorite tavern for farmers to stop at when in town. John Schmutz kept a tavern on Washington Street in the 1870's and 1880's. In the 1890's Nicholas Bergmeyer built the Columbia Hotel on Main Street. This was operated for several years by Milton Stevens and his sister, Belle, and later for many years by Mrs. Mollie Womack.

(Early names and dates were supplied by The Kentucky Historical Society, through Mr. Bayless Hardin.)

Banks

The Greenup Deposit Bank was founded probably in the late 1840's or early 1850's and was located on Harrison Street between Water (Front) and Elizabeth Streets. William Ireland was president and Joseph Pollock banker.

The Greenup Deposit Bank became the Citizens and later the First National. It was moved from the original site to its present home at Main and Harrison Streets when Edward Pollock became banker. This is now a branch of the Russell Bank, with a recently established branch at South Shore.

The Farmers and Merchant Bank was established by James Sowards at the present site of the Dr. Henry Morris home at Main and Washington Streets.

Industrial Development (1956)

Greenup County has progressed far from the early years of farming, milling and iron making, and from the later ones of cooper shops in the 1870's and a chair factory in the 1880's. With the coming of railroads, industrial development began in the northern part of the county.

In 1919, the King Powder Plant was built by a Cincinnati company at Wurtland, near the site of the old Fulton Forge and Oil Works of the 1850's and 1860's. This plant employs about forty men.

In 1926, the Graselli Chemical Plant was built at Wurtland by the DuPont Company of Delaware. Materials for both of these plants are shipped from elsewhere.

The Armco has extended quite a distance from Boyd into Greenup County, having purchased much land from the Poage family.

[50]

The C. & O. R.R. is expanding at Raceland, having bought land from the Powell family.

In 1895, Clyde King established a brick plant on the south side of Coney Island. This was in operation for several years. In 1904, the Charles Taylor Company of Cincinnati bought a part of the original Morton land from the Gray family. Here they built a fire-brick plant. This is known locally as the Taylor brickyard. When first operated, clay was brought from Shultz and Tygart over a tramway built along Tygart Creek. Kyanite, one basic raw material used in the products of the plant, is imported from India. Bricks from this plant are shipped to many foreign countries. The year 1956 saw the plant expanding in many ways, and a meeting brought together representatives from the United States, Canada and Mexico.

In the year 1956, a refractory plant was built at Siloam by the Esso-Ramtite Company. The firm purchased fifteen acres of land from James Wheeler, which was a part of the old Robert Johnson farm. The Esso-Ramtite Company will manufacture refractory plastics.

In 1956, the Chesapeake and Ohio Realty Company bought the farm of R. O. Judd and adjoining land from Robert Lawson. This land was sold to the Columbia Gas Company for the erection of a gas plant.

In 1944, the Chesapeake and Ohio Railroad built the "Overhead" to take the place of the White Oak Crossing. This begins at Jefferson Street in Greenup and extends through Riverton.

In 1954, the By-Pass, a new highway, was completed. This begins a half mile west of Greenup, crosses Little Sandy by a fill, follows Seaton Avenue, curves at Riverton and joins the main highway above the Overhead.

Greenup County is well supplied with gas by-lines from Texas and Tennessee. A new line laid in 1956 makes four that pass through land lying west of Greenup. Two of these are near Gray's Branch, one at Big Rocky and a fourth at Frost, all crossing the Ohio River. The headquarters for the Tennessee Company are located at Load, in Greenup County.

In 1956, several suits were filed against Russell residents condemning lands to permit the construction of U.S. Route 23 from West Russell to the Overpass in East Russell.

The Greenup County Park has been improved by the erection of poles, lights, paint and the enlargement of the horse-show ring. This was done under the sponsorship of the County Fair Association and made possible by contributions of the major industries of the county.

That year, too, new steel benches were placed, by the Fiscal Court, on the Court Square. Sponsored by the South Shore Lions Club, twenty-four street-markers were placed at the main intersections of that town. Streets east and west are from First to Fifth, avenues are Matilda, Hammond, Wheeler, Holly and Morton Lane. Others will be added later.

Projects (1956)

The Greenbo Lake project was launched in 1954 by citizens of Greenup and Boyd Counties, as a place of recreation, to be financed by popular subscription. This became a state project in 1956.

In 1956 the Greenup Improvement Association had four projects. The Lions Club under Lewis McCubbin planned to complete the road in the Riverview Cemetery. A second project was the construction of a Youth's Center by the Junior Chamber of Commerce under A. P. Bennett, president of the Jaycees. This project is under construction in East Greenup on land donated by Mrs. Carrie C. Morris. A third project was the beautification of the courthouse lawn. The Woman's Club was asked to undertake this work. The courtyard is now covered with grass and benches have been placed for people to use. A fourth project was to incorporate Riverton as a part of Greenup. This has been laid over until another time.

VI

Industries

Early Industries

THE GREATER number of Virginia pioneers that settled in Greenup County were farmers, and farming has always been the principal industry, producing now, as then, crops of corn, wheat, rye and oats, providing food for man and beast. Handmills were a part of every household for the grinding of meal, hominy and a coarse flour.

With the production of more grain, grist mills were built on the banks of Little Sandy River, Tygart, and other creeks suitable for the purpose. Farmers began raising more cattle, hogs, sheep and poultry for their own use and some to spare for their less fortunate neighbors. The wives and children of these pioneers were not sitting idly by, but each member of the family had a part in the weaving, sewing, knitting and other household chores. Also each had a part in using the hoe, shearing the sheep, milking the cows, helping to harvest crops and many other things that women of today know very little about.

The grist mills were replaced later by grain and lumber mills. Among these were the Myers mill on Town Branch in Greenup, the Hoop Mill at Argillite, the Womack Mill at Oldtown and the Bennett and Cooper Mills on Tygart Creek. Other industries were a cooper shop built in the early 1880's by Pratt and Brooks in the west end of the town, between Elizabeth and Main Street, for the purpose of making barrels to hold the molasses made from cane raised extensively by farmers along Little Sandy River. A cooper shop, operated by Alvin Morton, was in existence in the 1890's. The Myers mill was bought by the Robert Wilson family in 1880 and burned in 1888. It was rebuilt in 1889 on Harrison Street.

Agriculture

Farming was the principal industry in the county in the early days, corn, wheat, oats and rye being the main crops raised. Also, farm animals, horses, mules, cattle, sheep and hogs were produced. As the main crops raised took fertility from the soil and farm stock did not produce nearly enough manure, the farmer would clear more land for new crops. This was not too bad as land was plentiful and cheap and the farmer cleared his own land.

About 1880 farmers began raising more cattle and sheep, also more corn and wheat. When in the 1920's motor vehicles and machinery, electricity and telephones came into use, the farmer began to improve his methods of farming. While horse-drawn machinery has remained in some sections, it is fast losing to motor-driven machines.

In 1927 the County Fiscal Court employed a farm agent for the county, the first one being D. B. Redman, who served the farmer for five years. During these years a plan for the Extension Program was begun. For two years there was no agent. In 1934 Robert Wigginton was employed and during this time the Agriculture Adjustment Administration (AAA) was organized. During this time the 4-H movement was started and sixteen clubs were organized in the county, hybrid seed corn was being tested and farmers commenced spreading phosphates and lime and sowing lespedeza. William D. Kleiser was employed in 1938. Much emphasis was placed on sheep raising. This year, also, Miss Nancy H. Wilson came to the county to form groups of farm women to study improved methods of homemaking. This, under succeeding "Home Demonstration" agents, has developed into the Home Makers Club. John Irvin was employed as agent in the 1940's and during this time a great deal of swamp land was drained and ponds dug for use in pastures for the greater raising of livestock.

(The Census Bureau counted 920 farms in the county in 1960.)

Water Grist Mills

As Greenup County became more thickly settled and more grain was produced for food, the primitive method of grinding became too slow and laborious. Water grist mills began to be erected along the banks of Little Sandy River and Tygart Creek. As early as July 10, 1804, Jacob Kouns made application for the erection of a "Water Grist Mill on the Little Fork of Sandy." To do this, an application had to be made to the Court, a writ of *ad quo damnum*[1] issued to the sheriff, who summoned a jury for the purpose of deciding what damage might result from such a grant.

1. As to what damage might result from such a grant.

This first jury was composed of men whose descendants live in this and adjoining counties. The names of some of them were Joseph Powell, Josiah Davidson, Robert Poage, William Lowery, Jeremiah Stratton, and Andrew Hood.

February 15, 1806, Andrew Hood made application "concerning proposed establishment of a Water Grist Mill on the east fork of Little Sandy." Several names contained on the jury list were John Howe, John Craycraft, John Warnock, and Jesse Craycraft. On February 16, 1807, John Young made application "concerning the erection of a Water Grist Mill on Sandy" (at Palmyra). On May 25, 1809, Kinsey Virgin applied at Oldtown, and Richard Deering just below Hopewell. Early applications for the water grist mills on Tygart Creek were made by William Fuqua, August 30, 1810; by Thomas Waring, March 18, 1811, "at a place called Rocky Ford"; another by James Osburn "at Kentons on Tygart Creek."

Not all of these applications were granted for various causes, some being located in places that might cause damage to others. (Note: Bayless Hardin of the Kentucky Historical Society.)

Cattle raising became an important industry in the county and tanneries were constructed for tanning hides. Tanneries were built at Lynn, at Springville, Greenup and Oldtown. The hides were used in making shoes, boots, harnesses and saddles. In the 1840's a small shoemaking business was operated at Lynn which lasted long enough to give the name to the present community. The name was probably given for Lynn, Massachusetts, famous for its shoe factories.

The foundry on Elizabeth Street was an important early industry, as was a cotton mill in the west end of the town. When it did not prove profitable, the machinery was sold to John and Dan Young, who took it to Concord (Wheelersburg), Ohio, for use in a woolen mill.

Furnaces

Early settlers found the land rich in iron ore, and, with materials at hand, men from Pennsylvania became interested in the building of furnaces. Machinery for the building of them was brought down the Ohio River from Pittsburgh. In 1818, Richard Deering began the smelting of ore on his farm west of Hopewell (present) on the Little Sandy River. He built a small forge for the purpose of experimenting, which proved to be successful. He formed a partnership with David and John Trimble for the construction of a furnace at Argillite, which was the first iron furnace in the county. The industry grew and, during the years from 1818 to 1856, there were seventeen furnaces operating in the county. After the Civil War, the industry deteriorated and for years there were stacks of "pigs" in various parts of the county. The Hunnewell, the last in the county, blew out in 1881. On its last day the whistle blew from sunrise to sunset. The day was described by an "old-timer" as follows: "We stood, my fellow laborers and I, in reverence as the last whistle grew faint in the evening twilight. Many stood at attention with hats off. With the coming of night the last whistle died. The iron age had ended in Greenup County."

The furnace was a large pyramid of stone about twenty-five feet at the base and from twenty-five to forty feet high. It was built against a hill, so that the ore, limestone and charcoal could be dumped into the stack at the top, the molten iron being drawn from an outlet at the bottom. The ironmaster's home was built near the furnace. Other buildings near were storage sheds, carpenter and blacksmith shops and stables for horses and mules. The houses for families were built near, and schools for the employees' children. Employees were smelters, potters, guttermen and fillers at the furnace, and in the woods were the choppers who felled and trimmed the trees and corded the wood for the colliers to prepare the burning, which usually required from three to ten days, according to the nature of the wood used. Remains of the furnace stacks may be seen at Laurel and Raccoon. Charcoal burning continued for some years in the county, the product being shipped by barge and in high wagons, drawn by oxen, to Ironton Mills.

In the 1840's William W. Tong came to Greenup County and settled at what became known as Limeville where a small lime kiln had been operated by the Duval family. Mr. Tong enlarged this and originated the "Limeworks." It was a thriving business for many years, lime being shipped by river to Pittsburgh and Cincinnati. In the early 1900's a crusher was installed by William Merrill, the stone being used by the Chesapeake and Ohio Railroad.

A List of the Old Charcoal Furnaces of Greenup County from 1818-1881

Argillite	1818	Richard Deering
		John Trimble
		David Trimble
Old Steam	1824	Shreve Brothers
Pactolus	1824	McMurty and Ward

Bellefonte	1826	A. Paul and George Poage
Amanda	1829	Lindsay Poage
Enterprise	1832	Clingman and others
Hopewell	1832	John Campbell and others
Caroline	1833	Henry Blake and Co.
Raccoon	1833	David Trimble
New Hampshire	1838	Samuel Seaton and Co.
Hunnewell	1844	Campbell, Peters and Co.
Sandy	1847	Young and Gilruth
Pennsylvania	1848	Wurts Brothers
Laurel	1848	Wurts Brothers
Buffalo	1851	Hollister and Ross Co.
Kenton	1856	John Waring and others

(Taken from an article "Iron Industry" by Kendall Seaton.)

New Industries

Farm lands of Siloam and Frost are rapidly becoming industrialized. In 1958, the Columbia Gas Company built a plant at Frost, and is adding to the original plant.

In 1959, a plant for the manufacture of plastic brick was constructed at Siloam. The Hooker Chemical Company of New York commenced the erection of a plant at Siloam in 1961, for manufacturing plastic products.

The Tennessee Gas Transmission Company's pipelines that cross the Ohio below the Greenup high lift dam are threatened with erosion. Huge rocks are being dumped on the spots to halt this. It is planned to build towers on both sides of the river to hold the pipes, which must be high enough to offer no interference with traffic, according to river engineers.

VII

Transportation

Roads

IN THIS day of excellent highways and motor vehicles, it is difficult to realize there was a time when there were no roads at all in Greenup County. Pioneer overlanders from Virginia and Carolina were a brave and hardy people, brave to face an unknown land of forest and canebrake where Indians or wild animals could be lurking, to cross deep rivers, often traveling a long distance in order to find a fording place; hardy to have endured the many hardships encountered as they traveled, often wet, cold, and hungry, yet pushing on to an unknown destination, hoping for a better tomorrow.

When the pioneer found his destination and prepared some sort of habitation, his attention turned toward a roadway to others, if possibly there were any. This was an easy matter if families traveled together and settled near each other. After a while it became the duty of every man to give some of his time to road working. Later a tax was laid on the head—a poll tax—to be paid by work on the road under an overseer. This continued until road building became the business of the county and state, and at the present time we have a fine system of highways and byways with very few places that cannot be reached by cars and trucks.

Those people living today and who traveled the roads of the past three decades can remember the condition of them at that time, when only the streets of the town were paved with brick. Knowing the condition of county roads in the decades mentioned, one may realize what earlier ones may have been. We may well give a thought to the faithful doctors of those days, when they, as well as the farmers, wore leather boots that reached to the knees. The travel in winter had to be on foot or horseback. With the coming of automobiles in the early 1900's better roads were demanded and built and so today we have a fine system of highways.

Today we may see an occasional horse and small wagon on the highway, but no mules or oxen as in the older days.

Bridges

The bridges of the pioneers were made by felling trees along the banks of the streams and creeks. These answered the purpose of foot travelers, but were not for those who traveled on horseback or by wagon on reaching streams too deep or sandy for fording. With plenty of lumber near it was not a difficult matter for the pioneer with his all-important tool, the ax, to build a bridge where necessary. As the county became more thickly settled better bridges were constructed, many of them with roofs to protect the timbers. These were in use over Little Sandy River and Tygart Creek for many years. There were bridges also at the mouth of the Little Sandy River, at Coal Branch, at Rocky, and one at Enterprise which disappeared with its name but a few years ago.

These wooden bridges served their purpose well until the coming of the railroad when longer, stronger and more durable ones had to be constructed over wide streams and rivers. Iron bridges, and later, steel ones, were constructed over these and cement came into use for building smaller ones. An exception to these latter ones is the beautiful long cement bridge connecting Greenup and Boyd Counties. There are but two covered wooden bridges located in the county, one of these crossing Tygart at Bennett's Mill, and one on Upper Tygart, not far from the Carter County line. When the road was changed in the late 1920's from Sand Hill to Tygart, a new bridge was built in 1929, nearer the mouth, and the old iron bridge, built in 1857, was dismantled and rebuilt near Booton's Ford. This has never been of service because of the poor approach. This bridge may have been the first, or the second, iron bridge of the county, the other being the one connecting Greenup and Boyd Counties.

Two bridges connect Greenup County with Ohio, one, the Russell-Ironton Bridge, constructed in 1923. The other, the Portsmouth-Fullerton Bridge, was constructed in 1927.

The Ohio River

The Ohio River played a most important part in the settlement of Greenup County. History has told us of the Indian paddling his birchbark canoe over it and of the explorations of Col. George Croghan and Christopher Gist in 1757 and in 1775, of the coming of the flatboats down the river carrying families and "belongings" from old lands to the new. We have read of those eastern men[1] who formed a company, in 1810, for the building of boats, at Pittsburgh and of the first steamboat, the *Orleans,* launched there in 1811, which made a successful trip to New Orleans. Jo boats, john boats, skiffs, barges and ferries were in use for crossing to Ohio until the construction of the Russell-Ironton, and South Portsmouth Bridges.

With the coming of the Chesapeake and Ohio Railroad through the county, river travel and traffic declined sharply. Beginning in the 1860's and until 1900 there were many beautiful side-wheel passenger boats and many less beautiful but equally useful towboats plying the river constantly. There were many stern-wheel boats carrying both passengers and freight. Of the side-wheel boats the aristocrats were the *Fleetwood* and *Bostona.* These carried only through passengers and special mail. The *Potomac* and *Bonanza* were almost palaces, but the *Telegraph* with its beautiful whistle was the most popular boat of all. There was a succession of *Telegraphs*—all the same pattern. No. 7, which had been placed in the Louisville-Cincinnati trade, was wrecked near Louisville in 1897 and the beautiful whistle was lost.

No passenger steamboats and very few steam towboats ply the Ohio River today. There may be progress but, certainly, there is no beauty in the diesels that travel the river today with heavily loaded barges through the dams that began construction in the 1920's. Dam No. 30, located below Greenup, is to be removed and a roller dam is under construction below the present one.

January 1, 1962: The Greenup high-level dam begun in June, 1958, is virtually finished with the removal of the cofferdam. Two fatalities occurred during the construction and, in February, 1961, a bridge, damaged by the high water, fell dropping a crane locomotive and other tools into the river.

Boats

The *Orleans* created great excitement among those living on the banks of the Ohio River. A second boat, the *Comet,* was launched at Pittsburgh and taken to New Orleans in 1814. In 1815, the *Vesuvius* was built and launched at Pittsburgh by Rob-

1. In December, 1810, a steamboat company for building boats on the Ohio River was organized by Robert Fulton, De Witt Clinton, Robert Livingston, Nicholas Roosevelt and Daniel Tompkins, all New York men.

It is said that Nicholas Roosevelt was on the *Orleans,* and had landed at Louisville, through the storm that formed the Kentucky Lake. From *Steamboats and Steamboat Men* by Captain Ellis P. Mace.

ert Fulton. The *Enterprise* was built at Pittsburgh and carried a load of ordnance south and was used for the transportation of troops, arms and ammunition for General Jackson's army. All of these boats had but one deck, with the boilers in the hold. The *Washington*, built at Brownsville, was the first double-deck steamboat, and had her boilers on the lower deck. She went to New Orleans, stopped at Louisville in October, 1816, and returned to Louisville in November, proving ability to make headway against the current. (Note: The above was taken from *Steamboats and Steamboat Men* by Captain Ellis P. Mace.)

Captain Wash Honshell organized the Cincinnati, Portsmouth and Big Sandy Packet Company in 1872 and, later in the 1870's the White Collar Line. During the 1870's and 1880's, the Bay brothers, William and George, formed a company and built a line of boats, among them the *Minnie Bay, City of Ironton, Lizzie Johnson* and *Fashion*. The *Fannie Dugan* was built by Captain John McCallister of Springville. The first towboat on the Ohio was the *Condor*.

The high-lift Greenup Dam is in its final stage with the removal of the smaller dams 27, 28, 29 and 30. Included in this huge project, the cost of which is $55,000,000, has been the relocation of bridges, culverts, sewers and drainage facilities, and the clearing of banks for many miles upstream. During all of the months of the construction of the dam but two fatalities have occurred.

Floods

The following record of flood crests in the Ohio River at Greenup for the past 116 years were given by William I. Myers.

1832—61.5 Feet	1910—59.0 Feet	1939—57.2 Feet
1847—60.6 Feet	1913—67.0 Feet	1940—60.4 Feet
1883—59.4 Feet	1927—56.9 Feet	1943—59.11 Feet
1884—66.8 Feet	1933—59.9 Feet	1945—63.9 Feet
1897—57.9 Feet	1936—62.7 Feet	1948—64.1 Feet
1907—69.8 Feet	1937—73.8 Feet	

The following news of the 1883 flood was taken from a copy of the *Greenup Gazette*—Extra—dated February 15, 1883, which was loaned by Mrs. Frank Gettles of Jackson, Ohio:

"We are unable this week on account of the flood to present our readers with the regular issue of the *Gazette*. (Editor) . . . Under the title 'Refuge' we will give some of the highlights of the flood in this (a later) issue. Heavy rains in the Ohio Valley brought the river to a higher stage than at any time since 1847. All roads leading to town are flooded. Little Sandy Bridge is under water and the homes of William Warnock, Judge James Bryan, James Hockaday, and the Rankin Family are flooded. The families on West Main and on Perry Streets were moved to the second stories of stores, homes and to the courthouse and school buildings. On Saturday the river began to fall but Sunday began to rise again and buildings located on upper Front Street were flooded with damage to the Kouns House, the Spaulding home, which had been purchased by the Alvin Morton family and the Myers property. Little Sandy River Bridge was badly damaged." (Note—In the flood of 1884 the bridge floated away and the present iron bridge was begun the same year.)

Ohio River and Chesapeake and Ohio Railroad

The Ohio River played a very important part in the construction of the Chesapeake and Ohio Railroad between Huntington and Cincinnati. When this road entered Huntington from the east in 1873, Collis P. Huntington, the moving factor in its building, began to make plans for its extension to Cincinnati. Mr. Huntington contacted Captain Wash Honshell, of Catlettsburg, who was president of the famous White Collar Line of boats plying the river in the 1870's, who agreed to furnish two boats for the purpose of carrying passengers and freight between Cincinnati and Huntington. These boats were the *Fleetwood* and *Potomac*. During these years a new *Fleetwood* was built and the *Potomac* was succeeded by the *Bostona*.

The *Fleetwood* and *Bostona* were the finest and fastest boats of the Line, and had been running from Cincinnati to Pomeroy, landing only at important towns. They bypassed Greenup but landed at Riverton, almost a mile above, it being the terminus of the Eastern Kentucky Railroad.

Years passed before the right of way was obtained, concessions made by the counties through which it must pass, the purchase of the Maysville and Big Sandy Railroad, begun years earlier and not finished, being in litigation several years. In 1883, work on the railroad was begun and in January, 1889, local trains were being used. In March trains were carrying passengers and freight. The *Fleetwood* and *Bostona* were returned to their original runs between Cincinnati and Pomeroy. About this time, Captains Honshell and C. M. Holloway gained control of the U.S. Mail Line.

The *Fleetwood* ended her days between Cincinnati and Louisville. Other boats of the White Collar Line in the 1870's and 1880's were the *Bonanza* and *Telegraph*.

Ferries

The first ferries were canoes made by the Indians of birch and other light woods which were easily hollowed by primitive means and were more easily portaged. The Indian canoe was rounded at both ends, turning easily, and was propelled by a paddle. The pleasure canoe of today is patterned after the Indian canoe.

When Col. George Croghan and Christopher Gist explored the Ohio and Scioto River Valleys in early 1700, they found at the juncture of these a settlement of French and Indians, who ferried them over these streams in canoes. With better tools than the Indians had possessed French traders made a canoe of heavier wood, which they called a pirogue and in which they could carry the furs obtained by trading with the Indians.

When settlers came to the Ohio and Scioto Valleys with tools for making homes from lumber, small boats modeled after the large flatboats that carried many of these settlers were made and known as jo or john boats. These were propelled by paddle or furnished with locks for oars. Later boats with pointed bows and square sterns, called skiffs, were built. Small craft furnished with motors are used today for both pleasure and utility.

Later both sides of the larger stream became more thickly settled, flatboat ferries came into use. These were operated by sweeps, which were large oars, propelled by manpower. Smaller ones called pushboats and moved by poles were in use on the smaller streams.

Within the bounds of Greenup County from the Big Sandy River to the Scioto River there has been some sort of ferry across the Ohio River wherever needed. A flatboat was operated at the mouth of the Big Sandy in the early 1800's by Horatio Catlett. Members of the Boynton family were the operators of a ferry that plied between Russell and Ironton, Ohio, at an early date. The *H. A. Mead,* operated by Benjamin Young for many years, was sold to the Chesapeake and Ohio Railroad Company in 1889 and was in service until the Russell-Ironton Bridge was completed in 1923. Early ferries in service between Russell and Ironton were the *Elwood,* operated by the Boynton family, and the *Eva,* operated by Captain Wayne Carner of Russell.

The first ferryman at Greenup was Reason Davis, who kept a hat shop on Water Street in 1813. In 1814 William Bradshaw was permitted by the county court to establish a ferry across the Ohio River. In 1816 James McGuire, who had built a log house on Lot No. 1, operated a ferry across the Ohio River. All of these were operated by manpower, as also were many of those mentioned later.

Near the mouth of the Little Sandy River a ferry was in service before 1810—operated by Thomas Richards, who lived in a "hewed log house" on Water Street. Benjamin Smith, son of Godfrey Smith of Smith Branch, bought "Ferry Lot 11" and operated the ferry. Alexander Rankins, who owned the land west of Little Sandy River, was probably the last ferryman as at the December term of court 1851 it was "ordered that Benjamin Rankins be allowed the sun of $10 for ferrying the grand jurors and militiamen for the past year." It was about this time that the covered wood bridge, destroyed by the 1884 flood, was built.

In 1813 James Van Bibber was given "permission to establish a ferry below the Little Sandy Falls." The Van Bibber farm was beyond the Falls, where also a grist mill operated. Richard Deering was "permitted to establish a ferry from the lands of said Richard Deering to Lowry's Falls on the opposite shore." He was also granted "permission to erect a grist mill." Here also were Deering Salt Works, from where a pushboat poled salt down the Little Sandy for storage until shipped on a flatboat to New Orleans.

On the large streams manpower was succeeded by horsepower, using a treadmill. This was an appliance producing motion by the weight of a horse walking on moving steps which were connected with a revolving wheel.

The methods named above were in operation until about 1850, when steam engines came into use. At Greenupsburg a steam ferry was operated between the town and Haverhill, Ohio, in the 1860's. In 1890 the *Royal* was destroyed by ice and the ferryman, George Sanders, was drowned.

In 1857 the Kouns-Winn family had the ferry franchise and Major John C. Kouns and Joshua Oakers were made "Ferry Keepers." In 1890, Captain George Winn placed the *Thomas O'Neil* in the trade, where it remained until 1893 when Captain Winn took it to Fullerton and ran it between there and East Portsmouth. It sank in 1895, and a temporary boat was used until 1900, when the *B. F. Bennett*, which was being built at Point Pleasant, was finished. In 1902 Captain Winn died, and the *Bennett* was operated by Captain George Davis and his sons until his death, when Capt. John Davis took it over. The *B. F. Bennett* was replaced by the *Emily* and later by the *Captain John*. Because of lack of traffic the ferry was discontinued in 1952.

William Dupuy, in 1813, operated a ferry from Springville (South Portsmouth) and Portsmouth. He built a flatboat forty feet long and fifteen feet wide. John Mackoy became owner and operator of this ferry until his death in 1842, when his son, Thomas Mackoy, inherited the ferry. Members of the Mackoy family operated the ferry here until 1870. At this time the ferry had progressed from man to horsepower and to steampower. Captain W. W. Little became owner of the ferry, and it was named the *W. W. Little*. In the early 1880's Captain Little sold out to Captain Sam Brown, who named it the *Susie Brown*. In 1890 Captain Brown sold out to the Chesapeake and Ohio Railroad Company, and it was continued in the trade until the U. S. Grant Bridge was opened to traffic in 1927.

Ferries have gone the way of the palatial steamboat, freight boats and other river craft within the bounds of Greenup County as also have the horse-drawn buggy, carriage, stagecoach and wagon that were ferried across the streams. Diesel boats for transportation of coal and oil and some remaining towboats travel the river for business, while motor boats, canoes, and an occasional skiff skim along on pleasure bent. And one has a nostalgic yearning for those early days.

The Chesapeake and Ohio Railroad

The first Chesapeake and Ohio Railroad train ran from Huntington, W. Va., to Cincinnati, Ohio, December 26, 1889. Regular operation of train service began January 1, 1890. The fulfillment of rail transportation along the Ohio River brought into reality plans that had engaged the attention of northeastern Kentucky since 1850, when on December 18 an act was approved by the general assembly of the Commonwealth of Kentucky, to incorporate the Maysville and Big Sandy Railroad Company. This road was to be constructed from Maysville to the Big Sandy River "by such route as may be found practicable." Commissioners of Greenup County were Charles Wilson, John C. Kouns, William Corum and George Darlington. In April 1853 land and the ferry operating between Springville, Ky., and Portsmouth, Ohio, were bought, and rights of way were purchased. Plans for the road never matured and all rights became eventually the property of the Chesapeake and Ohio Railroad.

We show a picture of the first train to pass through Greenup County. The picture was made at Limeville, Kentucky. Frank Loring was the engineer, Martin Wilson the fireman, and George Winn the brakeman. R. E. L. Wilson was in charge of the commissary. Collis P. Huntington and President M. E. Ingalls, of Cincinnati were aboard.

The first woman passenger was Mrs. Mary Bennett Merrill of Limeville who traveled on the caboose to Greenup.

On May 2, 1888, a locomotive appeared at Springville, working from Ashland down.

June 16, 1888. Work on the road had passed through Maysvill 13 miles—at the rate of one mile a day.

January 5, 1889. Regular trains began running on the Chesapeake and Ohio.

May 13, 1889. The *F.F.V. (Fast Flying Virginian)* passed through Springville at 1:30 P.M. on the Chesapeake and Ohio Railroad.

The Eastern Kentucky Railroad

In 1865 the Kentucky Improvement Company was formed by Knapp, Thayer and Hunnel of Boston, Massachusetts. The company bought 25,000 acres of land at what is now Riverton (probably named by them) and south of it. A track to Hunnewell was laid in 1868. This became the Eastern Kentucky Railway Company in 1870, and the road was extended to Grayson by 1871 and to Webbville in 1873. In 1889 the length of the road was thirty-six miles, hauling pig iron from the furnaces to the Ohio River to be shipped by barge to Pittsburgh.

The first superintendent of the Eastern Kentucky Railroad was Mr. Goodwin of Boston. He was succeeded by H. W. Bates, whose son, Sturgis, was vice president and general manager until 1925, when the railroad was abandoned. James Schooly was the first engineer and Huey Craynon and Isaac Adams later ones. Conductors were Samuel Weaver and William McKee. Early station agents along the route were Charles Jacobs, Cread Milstead, Charles Weaver, John Irwin, Charles Eifort, Robert Leedy, H. K. Woods, and William Ostenton.

(Note: There is a picture of William J. McKee, conductor, and Brady Callihan, engineer, between pages 96-97.)

The following items are taken from a copy of the *Greenupsburg Independent* of May 25, 1871. "Nearly completed: It will be seen from the letter given below that cars are now running on the E.Ky.R.R. to Hopewell, four and one half miles beyond Hunnewell, and that the road will be completed to Grayson by June first.

"General Office Eastern Ky.R.R.Co.
"Riverton, Ky., May 23, 1871.
"George A. Creel—Dear Sir:
"Our regular train is now making one trip daily over the new road, as far as Hopewell, arriving there at 10:45 A.M. and leaving at 11 A.M. for Hunnewell. The time of the evening trip has not been changed.
"The track will be laid to Pactolus by the day of your issue, and to Grayson on or before June 1st.

"Yours truly,
"J. L. Staughton,
"J.M.C."

VIII

Education

1798   The Kentucky Legislature passed an act, which provided for the purchase of land and the erection of a school building in existing counties for the purpose of teaching academic subjects.

1803   Greenup County was organized.

1810   A special act was passed to establish an academy in Greenup County, to be under the supervision of three trustees.

1815   Land was purchased on Perry Street and a long, narrow brick building of two stories, two rooms, two halls with two front doors facing Perry Street was erected. This was painted gray.

1835   The academy was changed to a public school but known until 1880 as Greenup Academy.

1843   The three trustees were succeeded by three commissioners.

1880   The commissioners were succeeded by a Superintendent of County Schools. Two new rooms were added to the Academy and several years later, two more rooms with a basement were added. The building was painted red.

1937   The school building was badly damaged by the flood of 1937. It was razed and the present commodious one was erected. Within the past thirty years high schools have been constructed at Greenup, Russell, Raceland, Wurtland, McKell and South Portsmouth.

(A list of commissioners, superintendents and of many early teachers may be found in *A History of Greenup County*, as well as many interesting things about early schools and teachers.)

THE SUBJECT of consolidation of schools had been under discussion for several years and came to a head in the year 1956. The work was begun under the supervision of the county superintendent, Roscoe Stevens, who was elected in 1954. Brick buildings, each containing eight rooms, were to be erected at Oldtown, Argillite, Grays Branch, McKell, Sunshine, Lynn, Warnock, East Fork and Wurtland.

Before 1906 there were five school districts in the County. These were Greenup, Russell, Fullerton, South Portsmouth and Advance. The first grade school was organized at Greenup, in 1882. The first high school was organized at Russell in 1913. Before 1900 there were twenty-seven frame and thirty-two log buildings. In 1930, there were fourteen brick and seventy-seven frame buildings. The last log building disappeared in 1912 (Fred Maynard).

The year 1956 saw many of the one- and two-room buildings being sold at auction, some being retained for possible use. The following notice has appeared several times in the local newspapers: "The Greenup Board of Education will, at the times and places noted here, offer for sale at public auction the below described school buildings which are now the property of the Greenup County Board of Education."

School Commissioners

1841-1843	Basil Waring, William Dupuy and John Culver
1844-1846	M. Warnock, J. Davidson and Marshall Baker
1847-1849	J. Davidson, William Corum and Samuel Seaton
1850-1852	E. J. Honaker
1853-1855	L. D. Ross
1856-1858	Robert Galbraith
1859-1862	J. Davidson
1863-1866	Robert Galbraith
1867-1869	F. B. Trussell
1870-1871	S. J. Filson
1872-1874	S. H. Walcott
1875-1878	J. W. Womack
1878-1880	W. H. Clifton
1881-1883	J. B. Norris
1884-1885	F. B. Trussell
1885-1886	W. H. Clifton
1886-1890	Charles Smith, first superintendent
1890-1898	L. R. McCarty
1898-1902	J. M. Literal
1902-1910	L. F. Thompson
1910-1914	J. G. Pritchard
1915-1918	Sophia Kitchen
1918-1925	J. N. Hatfield
1925-1929	R. J. Nickell
1929-1930	Mrs. R. J. Nickell
1930-1932	Robert Nickell
1932-1933	Jesse Stuart
1933-1938	Fred Maynard
1938-1942	W. Tong West
1942-1950	Fred Maynard
1950-	Roscoe Stevens

Greenup Academy

The following copy of "A Catalogue of the 1878-1879 sessions of the Male and Female Academy of Greenup County, Kentucky" was loaned by Mrs. Frank Gettles, of Jackson, Ohio, who is a daughter of Mrs. Belle York (deceased).

The First Session commences on the First Monday in September. The Second Session commences on the First Monday in February.

THE INDEPENDENT PRESS, GREENUP, KY., 1878

Board of Trustees   Dr. A. D. DeBard   C. L. Hertel   B. F. Pratt

Teachers

Professor S. T. Kenyon, Principal and Teacher of the High School
Mrs. Charles Van Bibber, Teacher of the Intermediate Department
Miss Anna Davidson, Teacher of the Primary Department

— Course of Study —

Primary Department—Reading, First, Second and Third Readers, Written and Mental Arithmetic, Spelling, Punctuation and Penmanship.
Intermediate Department—Fourth, Fifth and Sixth Readers, Arithmetic, Spelling, Penmanship, Grammar, Geography and United States History.
High School. First Year—Higher Arithmetic, Advanced Grammar, Physical Geography and Ancient History.
Second Year—Algebra, Natural Philosophy, Chemistry and Universal History.
Third Year—Geometry, Rhetoric, Physics, Literature and Political Economy.
Fourth Year—Trigonometry, Geology, Physiology, Criticism and Logic.
Elective Branches—Latin, Greek, German and French by special teachers at additional expense.

Boarding may be had at $2.00 to $3.00 per week. Total expenses need not be over $15.00 per month. There are two Methodist Churches, one Presbyterian and one Christian Church in the town.

A Literary Society is connected with the Academy.

HIGH SCHOOL DEPARTMENT

NAMES	RESIDENCE
Agnew, Effie	Quincy, Ky.
Bryan, Jennie	Greenup, Ky.
Davidson, Anna	Greenup
Gray, Venia	Duval's Landing, Ky.
Ghent, Laura	Greenup, Ky.
Jones, Zora	Galena, Ohio
King, Gertrude	Greenup, Ky.
Oakes, Ona	Haverhill, Ohio
Pfaff, Mary	Greenup
Pfaff, Carrie	Greenup
Roe, Alice	Greenup
Roe, Lucy	Greenup
Rankins, Kate	Greenup
Van Bibber, Ratie	Greenup
Winn, Sallie	Greenup
Womack, Mary	Oldtown, Ky.
York, Belle	Greenup, Ky.
York, Sallie	Greenup, Ky.
Biggs, William	Smith Branch, Ky.
Biggs, John	Smith Branch, Ky.
Brush, Benjamin	Haverhill, Ohio
Crawford, William	Riverton, Ky.
Clark, James	East Fork, Ky.
Davidson, W. A.	East Fork, Ky.
Ellis, Samuel B.	Greenup, Ky.
Hager, Charles	Greenup, Ky.
Kendall, Travis	Oldtown, Ky.
Oakes, Oliver	Haverhill, Ohio
Pratt, Edward	Greenup, Ky.
Pollock, Joseph	Greenup, Ky.
Rankins, Emmett	Greenup, Ky.
Scott, Henry	Laurel Furnace, Ky.
Warnock, Horace	Greenup, Ky.
Walcott, William	Greenup, Ky.
Worthington, Finley	Raccoon Furnace, Ky.
Womack, John	Oldtown, Ky.
Womack, Charles	Oldtown, Ky.

INTERMEDIATE

Barr, Sallie
Callihan, Hattie
Mitchell, Maud
Mitchell, Nina
Roe, Nannie C.
Taylor, Minnie
Warnock, Anna
Winter, Sallie
Willis, Mary

Walcott, Viola
Woodrow, Gertie
Hoffman, John
Jacobs, Thomas
Kuchborth, Albert
McMullen, David
McMullen, Henry
Pratt, Thomas
Reed, John

Sellards, Howard
Sowards, William
Warnock, Edward
Willis, George

Winn, George
Woodrow, Albert
Riggs, James
Sowards, John

Woods, Charles

PRIMARY DEPARTMENT

Calliahan, Alice
Heltel, Laura
Mitchell, Gertie
Myers, Esther
Rankins, Ella
Pratt, Laura
Reed, Emma
Reed, Mary

Sellards, Maggie
Sellers, Sallie
Hertel, Samuel
Hollingsworth, Edward
Leewis, Benny
McMullen, Joseph
Mitchell, Clarence
Nickell, Charles

Puthuff, Henry

Teachers

The names of many of the early teachers of the county were printed in *A History of Greenup County*. The names of others have been obtained and are included in this edition of the history. As learned, they were: Charles Norris, Scott Clifton, Elmer Hood, Allen Berry, Frances Fullerton, Myrtle Hartley, Laura Rye, Minnie Cooper, Ella Chinn, Cora Warnock and Annie Hill. Teachers of the early 1900's were J. M. Literal, Sophia Kitchen, Alma Womack, Elmer Fullerton, Lillian Fullerton, Charles Secrest, Thad Hunt, Lena Hunt, Imogene Rardin, Edith Johnston, Nora Hertel, Nannie Boynton and Addie Downs.

For length of service and devotion to the cause of education, names remembered are Charles Norris, Kate Stark Virgin, B. F. Kidwell, Elizabeth Crawford and Addie Downs—all teachers of Greenup County. Beside Annie Davidson (Littlejohn), others who taught in the county in their early years were George Clark, who became principal of the Hindman School and taught until retired; Robert J. Nickell, teacher and superintendent, who has taught in Florida the past few years; B. F. Kidwell, principal at Russell for twenty-four years, and then at Catlettsburg, is a teacher of mathematics at McKell High; and Jesse Stuart, teacher, superintendent of schools, poet, writer and novelist. There are others who are too numerous to include in this sketch of teachers.

Private Schools

The Greenup Academy, built in 1815, remained a private school until 1835. In 1840, Charles Kingsbury of Boston, Massachusetts taught a private school at the Sam Seaton farm in the rear of the town. A Miss Pollock taught a private school in the town in the 1850's, as also did Miss Helen A. Seaton, of Maysville, in 1856 and 1857. Miss Mary E. Lyons taught a private school at Lynn in 1858.

When the George Wurts family bought the John McConnell farm at Wurtland in the 1860's, the law office was used as a school by the Wurts and Brammar children of Wurtland, the Collinses and Davissons of Ohio, and the Biggs and Stark children of Greenup. Mrs. Bruce King taught school at the home in what has since been known as Academy Hollow and was attended by the John Seaton and Jesse Corum children.

Other teachers of private schools have been Miss Mary E. Seaton, J. B. Norris, Mrs. Lola Morton and Rev. J. R. Pinkerton, a Christian Church minister.

John B. Norris was a private and normal school teacher in Greenup, during the years of 1870-1880. A private school was in session at the Norris home on Main Street. The normals, supplementing the public school, were held in the Academy. The latter were attended by many pupils from other places than Greenup, especially by those who were preparing for teaching. We have received a picture from G. B. Norris (Bert), son of Professor Norris, whose family moved to Columbus, Ohio, and which was made in 1876 or 1877. The names of those in the picture are Professor Norris, Tony Norris, and Anna Thom at the rear. In the front row are Sam Seaton, Will Sowards, George Sample, John Sowards, Dan Lacock and Tom Jacobs. The second row shows Bert Norris, Walter Hockaday, Georgia Womack and Lily Womack. In the third row are John Hoffman, Forest Womack, Dora Seaton, Grace Warnock and Bennella Norris; and in the fourth are Mary Schmutz, Edward Ghent, Harlan Womack, Nola Boyd, Irene Halbert, Mollie Seaton, Winfield Warnock and Russell McCallister. Many pupils attended Professor Norris' school through the year, while others attended only during vacation time. Other private schools were taught by various teachers. (Between pages 96-97.)

Memories of School Days

School life for me began in September, 1872, about a month before I was six years old. I remember that Monday morning well: I see my mother holding my pink-checked bonnet and me running around the baby's cradle to keep from having it on. However, I soon found the bonnet on my head, a small slate and a yellow-backed book in one hand, the other hand in my sister's, who had attended school the year before, as I was led to the Greenup Academy, where I was to obtain the greater part of my education. As the public term of school lasted but five months, we sometimes attended subscription schools taught by residents of the town in other buildings.

I found my first teacher to be a pretty dark-haired, dark-eyed young lady, Miss Davidson, from Ohio, who took off my bonnet and placed me in a seat with two other little girls. Without waiting to see what would follow, I proceeded to use my slate and pencil, drawing what I imagined was a bird. One of my little seatmates told the teacher I was making pictures. She told me to bring the slate to her, and she told me to show it to the children. I held it as she said until I got tired and went to my seat. I did not realize that I was being punished, but I lost my taste for drawing right then and there. The teacher and I became very good friends, occasioned, perhaps, by a young minister, who boarded at Grandmother's. They became interested in each other and there were many notes written, with my sister the carrier and me on the sideline.

I must have learned that yellow-backed *McGuffey Primer* well, for to this day I remember the last page, "The Ten Commandments" in rhyme. These were as follows:

> Thou no Gods shalt have but me.
> Before no idol bend the knee.
> Take not the name of God in vain.
> Do not the Sabbath Day profane.
> Give to thy parents honor due.
> Take heed that thou no murder do.
> Do not commit adultery.
> What is not thine let it be.
> Do not tell a lie nor love it.
> What is thy neighbor's do not covet.

We learned the alphabet by singing it.

> A B C D E F G
> H I J K L M N O P
> Q R S T U V
> W X Y Z.

Col. Wm. J. Worthington

Thomas H. Paynter

Joseph Bently Bennett

Joe B. Bates

Courtesy of George D. Corum

Jesse Stuart, poet and author and
Richard Cocchini, sculptor

Old Clerks Office and former Courthouse

Courthouse built 1811-16

Courtesy of George D. Corum

Methodist Church

Courtesy of George D. Corum

Christian Church

Presbyterian Church

The John B. Norris School (1876-87)

The Side-wheeler "New Orleans"
In 1811, this sturdy boat was the first to ply the
Ohio River

The "Fleetwood"
This was one of the last steamboats on the
Ohio in the decades 1870-1880-1890

Eastern Kentucky Railroad
Wm. J. McKee, Conductor
Hugh Craynon, Engineer

First Chesapeake and Ohio train through County

Covered Bridge built around 1850

In the Third Grade we were taught to distinguish the vowels from consonants by memorizing the following rhyme:

A E I O U

If I O U A E and I,
And sometimes W and Y,
It must be love that I O U
And love that U O I.

Also we learned, while in the Third Grade, the names and uses of the parts of speech, in rhyme, the first being:

Three little words we often see
Are Articles, A, An and The.

During those early years at the Academy, we had but three primary teachers, one of whom, Mrs. Van Bibber, taught for several years. Friday afternoons were given over to recitations, when the pupils were dressed in better, if not best, bib and tucker. As there were few books of poetry in the schools, most of the recitations were taken from the *McGuffey Readers,* the favorites being "Twinkle, Twinkle Little Star," "We Are Seven," "Mary Dow" and "The Guide Post." When promoted to the Fourth Grade, "Try, Try Again," "Meddlesome Matty," "Lazy Ned" and "The Tempest" were recited over and over again. Later favorites taken from the Fifth and Sixth Readers were "Rienzi's Address To The Romans," "Maud Muller," "Rock Me To Sleep" and "Lochinvar."

I remember so well many of the young ladies who were in the principal's room before we were promoted there. They wore pretty dresses that touched the floor, which they held up daintily. We admired them very much, and envied them too. Fashions had changed and long dresses for school wear had gone out of style.

Also, after the war, times became harder, and serviceable, instead of pretty, clothes were the order of the day. Memory recalls some of those older girls, and two especially, one of whom died of a broken heart and the other by her own hand.

In 1874, Professor Samuel T. Kenyon became principal of the Academy and he remained for five years. He did many things to improve the school, among them a system of ventilation, and purchasing a battery taught us the uses and power of electricity, something very new to us, which created a great deal of interest. Professor Kenyon organized that educational diversion, the Literary Society, with declamations, dialogues, spelling matches and debates. The Society was a common meeting ground for the pupils of the town and those from surrounding areas who attended the spring normal schools that began at the close of the five-month public school. During the two terms with Professor Kenyon our class studied McGuffey's Fifth and Sixth *Readers,* McGuffey's *Speller,* Ray's *Arithmetic, Mental and Written,* Harvey's *Grammar,* Barnes' *History* and Mitchell's *Geography,* with Algebra, Rhetoric, Latin and Physical Geography, which were added during the second term.

I do not remember seeing a pupil severely punished during my ten years attendance at the Academy. Of course pupils were punished in different ways, as I do remember one of the older boys supplying many of the younger pupils with "shooters," a thin, limber stick, and grains of corn. The sticks went into the stove and the corn confiscated, which ended that fun. Another time occurred when the Physical Geography Class was given a description of the aurora borealis to memorize. When the class was called all members could recite the description but my seat mate and I, not because we could not have learned it, but we did not think it was necessary. After losing both recesses and part of the noon hour one day, we changed our minds about learning the assignment.

After four terms of academic study and a normal term, I, and several of my schoolmates in 1882 passed a teacher's examination and were given certificates of teaching. Although I lacked almost one month of being sixteen years old, I obtained a three-month school, the last term ever taught at the site of what had been one of the most important furnaces. The large log school house was being used for a sheep farm and school was held in a room of an old log dwelling with but thirty-nine pupils.

After teaching four country schools, I married a farmer, which is another story.

The Town Band

The following poem was sent to the authors of *A History of Greenup County* too late to be included in the printing of the history.

Etta Hodges Salzman, a daughter of Harvey and Martha Smith Hodges, was reared in Greenup. The Hodges home was a cottage on the late where the McCubbin home stands, and faced Elizabeth

Street. Etta Hodges was quite a writer of news and poems for local publications. She was married to Edward Salzman, and lived in Cincinnati where she died in 1943.

The Little Home Town Band

The stirring notes of Sousa's band have often thrilled my ear,
    And I've heard the dreamy waltzes of Vassela—on the Pier.
I've heard the Polish pianist, Paderewski, pour his soul
    In notes of heavenly harmony that down the ages roll.
I have heard the birdlike strains of Galli Curci's golden voice,
    Caroling such sweet refrain that one's heart could but rejoice.
I have heard the great Caruso sing his arias so sublime,
    That in ecstasy I trembled—'twas so gloriously divine.
But the music that is sweetest, in memory to me—
    That wafts me back my childhood—unclouded and carefree,
Oh, the music that is sweetest in all of this great land—
    Is the memory of the music of my Little Home Town Band.
Ah, in fancy I can see them in uniforms so gay,
    As they proudly marched up Main Street on every holiday,
Led by "Schmitty," the drum major, whose towering chapeau
    Filled my childish heart with wonder in the long, long ago.
The Wilson boys, cornetists, God bless 'em, the three,
    "Chuck," "Mart" and "Bob"—each wonderful to me;
The drummer boys—the Mitchells and "Johnny" Kinsler, bass—
    I call them all to memory—each cherished name and face.
I can see them now, a-marching around the courthouse square,
    As "My Old Kentucky Home" made sweet the summer air.
And the children, white and colored—were always near at hand,
    To keep in step and listen to the Little Home Town Band.
So, the music that is sweetest in memory to me,
    That brings me back to my childhood—unclouded and
        carefree—
That brings back old loved faces—now in the other land—
    Is the memory of the music of my Little Home Town Band.

                        —Etta Hodges Salzman

The above poem was inspired by memories of the Greenup Cornet Band of the 1880's, member of which were John Smith, leader; Charles, Mart and Robert Wilson; Grant and Stanley Mitchell; Alfred and Charles Hager; George Winn; John Kinsler, Albert Woodrow; Thomas Peters and James Smith.

Old Sayings

These apt expressions or "old sayings" have come down through generations of families, each having its own special ones. Some of them may be "as old as the hills." Who knows when or by whom the Biblical expressions "meek as Moses," "patient as Job" or "wise as Solomon" were first used? My grandmother, who came from Virginia in the early 1800's had a plenteous store of "old sayings" and I find myself often using "as good as gold," "pretty is as pretty does," "easy come, easy go," "least said, soonest mended," "too farfetched," "kith and kin," "thick and thin" and others.

When teaching country schools and visiting among families I heard many others some of which were "fit as a fiddle," "sly as a fox," "gentle as a lamb," "dumb as an ox," "fat as a pig," "sweet as honey," "green as grass" and "black as pitch."

I married into a farm family who had their own particular brand of "old sayings'—"soft as silk," "light as a feather," "bitter as gall," "sharp as a tack," "blind leading the blind," "off on the wrong foot" and "third time the charm" being a few of them.

We used to have a neighbor, a farmer in our community, whose special "old sayings" were "twixt you and me and the gate post," "better be a big frog in a little puddle than a little frog in a big puddle" and "you never can tell by looking at a frog how far it can jump." As this is being finished many "old sayings" come to mind, but "enough is enough."

IX

Religion

EARLY SETTLERS from Virginia brought their religious beliefs to their new homes in Greenup County. These were embodied in Methodism, which originated in England, and Presbyterianism, originating in Scotland and Ireland.

In 1810, Samuel Demint, who is said to have been the first preacher in the new county, organized class meetings which were held in the homes of the Methodists, until buildings were provided for services. In Greenupsburg a small frame building was used until the present brick church was erected in 1845. At various places in the county, log meeting houses were built for services.

Prayer meetings were held in the homes of Presbyterians. At a meeting held in the home of a Poage family in 1819, a church was organized and a small log church built the same year, with twenty members. This was replaced in 1828 by a brick church built at another location. In 1858, the present brick church was erected at Ashland, Boyd County.

In 1829, at a prayer meeting in the John Lawson home, a Presbyterian church was organized and built the same year at Gray's Branch with ten families joining. This was named Greenup Union. In 1881, a new brick church was built, with the name changed to Brick Union. This church has become the property of a Christian congregation.

In 1859, a Presbyterian church was organized and built in Greenupsburg. Members who lived in town and attended services at the Greenup Union Church joined with the new church in the town. When for lack of members the Brick Union Church was abandoned, the few remaining joined with the Greenupsburg Church.

Church of Christ, or Christian, originated in this section of the county in the early 1830's. Many, through the preaching of Alexander Campbell, were organized in Kentucky. Probably the first one was organized at Siloam, in 1840. In 1850 the Christian

Church was organized and a brick church was built in 1855. In the early 1940's this church was razed and the present one built on the site.

There were few Baptist families and no Baptist churches in the early days of the county. Services were held in the homes. In the early 1900's many families began selling or leasing their land to coal, oil and gas companies and began moving to other counties, and many came to Greenup County. The Baptists among these built small frame houses for service, but in recent years have erected large buildings, those at East Greenup, Russell and South Shore being the most prominent ones.

Other religious organizations of recent growth are Nazarenes, Pentecostal, and Church of God, the last at South Shore. The Nazarenes have taken over churches outgrown by other congregations.

The Union Church, built at Wurtland in 1865, has become the property of the Methodists, and the Union Church built in the 1920's at Siloam is used by a Nazarene congregation at present.

Churches

Pioneers who settled Greenup County were, as a rule, religious people, and, before churches were built, met in the homes of the members to worship. Traveling preachers came to the settlements, but the first record of one living in the county reads, "In 1814, Samuel Demint produced credentials that he was in regular communion with the Methodist Society and was permitted to solemnize the 'rites of matrimony' according to the rules of said church." He organized several churches in the county, among them the Mount Zion and Oldtown about the same year (1820). He was pastor of the Mount Zion Church for six years. Other early preachers were Dan Young, ordained in New Hampshire, who preached church and funeral sermons in the county.

Early Methodist services were held in a building, called the "preaching house," which stood on the corner west of the present church, which was built in 1845 on Lot 27, donated by Mayor John C. and Elizabeth Smith Kouns. A Methodist church was built in 1880 on Perry Street, and was razed when the north and south churches united. The first church in Russell was the Mead Chapel, named for a member of the Mead family, Mrs. Belle Mead Pritchard, who gave time and financial support to its organization and building. Many Methodist churches have been organized over the county. About 1820, Samuel Demint organized a Methodist Society which met in a log building at Springville.

In 1876, the present church was built on land donated by Reuben and Elizabeth Thomson. In 1903, a church organized and built at Fullerton on land donated by Nannie Fullerton Holly was dedicated as a North Methodist Church. In 1939, the Fullerton Church became a part of the Ashland District. A brick church, serving both Fullerton and South Shore, is under construction at South Shore. A Methodist church at Bethlehem was built in 1892 on land donated by Thomas and Elizabeth Jane McNeal, and in 1909 a church was built at Limeville, on land donated by the Bennett-Merrill family.

A Presbyterian church was organized in the home of John Lawson at Gray's Branch, January 14, 1829, by Rev. Eleazer Brainard of the Portsmouth Presbyterian Church, and was known as the Greenup Union Presbyterian Church. In 1881, the name was changed to Brick Union when the present church was built. In 1919, the church was sold to the Christian congregation. The few members of the Presbyterian church transferred their membership to the Greenup Church. The Greenup Presbyterian Church was built in 1859 on land donated by the Kouns-Pollock family. (A Presbyterian church has been built recently in Flatwoods.)

A record of the Siloam Christian Church is in existence which shows that in 1819, the congregation met as the Regular Baptist Church of Tygart Creek. In 1834, evidently through the influence of the teachings of Alexander Campbell they embraced his doctrine and assumed the name of the Church of Christ of Tygart Creek. Minutes of meetings were signed by John Mackoy. In January 1840 the minutes state that a meeting was held at the Siloam Meeting House, probably built by Nicholas Fisher Thom, an elder of the church, on ground given by John Mackoy. This church burned in the early 1900's and the present church was built on the site.

The Christian Church in Greenup was organized and built in 1855 on land given by the Seaton-Spalding families. The church was razed in the early 1940's and the present building erected. Both churches were brick buildings.

Christian

A Christian Church was organized, October, 1854, near the Falls of Little Sandy by Moses F. Mackoy. Nicholas F. Thom was in charge of this church, which was a log building and was in use until the early 1900's for both church and school purposes. In 1855, when a Christian Church was erected in Greenup, the members of the Short Branch Church transferred their membership to it, although services continued to be held by Elder Thom at the Short Branch building. The following officials were chosen from both churches, in 1855, the elders being N. F. Thom, Alex Rankins, Frank York and John H. Sennett, and deacons John Hoffman, Frank H. Warnock, Benjamin Smith, Alex Patton and Samuel Kritzer.

In 1855, the Seaton, Spalding, Morton, Hockaday, and Ireland family names were added and later the Childerson, Mitchell, Powell Roe, Pratt and Halbert families became members. Later, the present brick building was erected on the site of the old, on Main Street, with the following committee in charge: A. B. Morton, M. J. Webb, D. S. Mitchell, C. F. Taylor, William Collins, C. B. Bennett, William Callihan, David Darby, Mrs. A. B. Morton and Dora Seaton. Early ministers were George E. Dorsey, Elder N. F. Thom and J. R. Pinkerton.

The Liberty Christian Church was organized and built in 1850 on land donated by Rival and Mary Fuqua Jones for, as they said, "as long as the sweet water flows and the green grass grows." The two frame churches have long since disappeared with only foundation stones to show their existence. Other Christian churches in the county are at Russell and at Fullerton. In recent years, Baptist churches have been built at different places in the county. Also, newer denominations have built churches at several places.

Teachers and Pupils of Greenup Christian Church School

(Courtesy of Mrs. Lucille Wilson Bennett)

Several names on the list were from the Presbyterian Sunday School which met Sunday afternoon.

1875

CLASS 1

George Hockaday, *Teacher*	Edgar Rye
Allen Myers	Cyrus Van Bibber
Clarence Lacock	B. E. Roe (Bud)
Frank Lacock	Ellis Powell
J. Lawrence McCoy	C. Callihan
Alex. Rankins	Don Judd

[82]

CLASS 2

J. W. Womack, *Teacher*
Ina Lacock
Ratie Van Bibber
Mary Jones
Irvin Hockaday
Samuel Ellis (Hal)
Ellis Hurn
Charles Hager
Marshall Halbert
Nellie Vincent
Mollie Roe
Joe Pollock
Anna Jones
Amanda Mackoy
Bird Jacobs
India Pratt

CLASS 3

Mrs. Spalding, *Teacher*
Bertie Halbert
George Halbert
Lucy Roe
Belle York
Dora Seaton
Sam Spalding
Ellen Hailey
E. Hockaday
Sam Seaton, Jr.
Will Worthington
Walter Hockaday
Lizzie Jones
Alfred Hager
Mollie Seaton

CLASS 4

J. B. Norris, *Teacher*
Helen Spalding
Rebecca Spalding
Ed Seaton
Harlan Womack
Forrest Womack
James Lacock
Howard Sellards
Emmett Rankins
John McCoy
E. Hertel, Jr.
Alf Hawkins
Ed. Pratt
Sam Bailey

CLASS 5

Hattie Powell, *Teacher*
Ben Powell
Mollie Willis
May Hockaday
Lula Walters
Mary Turk
Harry Ewing
Kate Rankins
Grant Mitchell
Nina Mitchell
Rene Halbert
Allie Powell
Nannie Roe
Stella Carr

CLASS 6

Nellie Vincent, *Teacher*
Thomas Hurn
Lily Womack
Grace Warnock
Mary Warnock
Anna Warnock
Myra Warnock
C. Rankins
Mandy Crisp
Mary Reeves
Sarah Reeves
Ellen Turk

CLASS 7

Mrs. Powell, *Teacher*
Hattie Carr
Charles Morford
India Callihan
Nellie Rankins
Nellie Ferguson
Annie Walters
P. Sanders
G. Sanders
Mary Reed
Gertie Mitchell
Lucy Halbert
Ed. Hollingsworth
Ollie Reeves

CLASS 8

Mrs. Mefford, *Teacher*
Dan Lacock
Nannie Hurn
L. Crisp
Thomas McCoy
George Sanders
Willie Hertel
John Reed
H. A. Warnock
Mollie Norris
Allen McCoy

Frank McCoy
Ella Hailey
Bertie Hailey

CLASS 9

Mrs. Norris, *Teacher*
Lucy Hockaday
Bennie Norris
Sallie Pratt
Hattie Callihan
Maggie Creqor
Mary Creqor

First Methodist Church of Russell

Mrs. E. W. Potter

The history of this church goes back to 1870, when Methodist Sunday School classes were held in the home of James Rayburn. The attendance increased greatly and services were transferred to the school house, which then stood on the site of the Dr. W. E. Potter home. For a few years services were conducted there by circuit riders. From 1874 to 1908, the church was a part of different circuits, with the pastor residing at Greenup or Flat Woods.

In 1887, Captain Carner gave land on Bellefont Street for the construction of a church which was soon completed. In 1921-1922 an addition was made to this church which was in use until 1929, when the present church, on Main and Etna Streets, was dedicated. Those who were in charge were the pastor, Rev. W. W. Shepherd; Rev. T. S. Henderson, E. R. Overly, A. W. Robinson, A. S. Morgan, C. S. England and B. S. Trent. Among liberal contributors were W. S. Butler and his associates.

In 1934, C. S. Patterson gave the pipe organ in memory of his wife. On October 31, 1948, an anniversary meeting was held at the church. Nine of the building committee of the First Methodist Church were living. These were A. S. Morgan, C. S. England, M. E. Collins, Dr. J. A. Franz, I. M. Gilley and F. C. Moore.

Rev. C. D. Harsh was pastor of the church for five years, 1948-1953. W. F. Fryman was the District Superintendent.

Liberty Methodist Church at Lynn

The Liberty Methodist Church was organized and built in 1850, on land donated by John and Ursula Waring. Trustees named in the deed were Moses Dupuy, Basil Waring, Edward Stevenson,

Charles Craycraft and J. S. Canterbury. This church, built of brick, was located near the Liberty Cemetery and burned in 1882. A new one, also of brick, was built on the banks of Tygart Creek and dedicated in 1887.

In 1946, this brick church was razed and the present one of concrete built on the site. Early members of the church, besides those mentioned above, were the Howland, Hardman, Van Bibber, Farmer, Stewart and Holbrook families. The first preacher was Hugh Rankin. At different times the Lynn Church has been on the Mount Zion, Springville and Greenup Circuit.

A Union Church was organized and built at Wurtland in 1860. It was presented to the community by George and Mary Ann Wurts as a place for Union worship, and has been used as such since that time.

Fullerton-South Shore Methodist Church

The first church was organized in the new village of Fullerton in 1902 when a group of Methodists met in a small frame school building that stood on the east part of the lot, occupied later by the large frame building on Main Street. Charter members were Mr. and Mrs. James Fullerton, Mr. and Mrs. Edward McCall, Mr. and Mrs. Henry Ruel, Mrs. Maggie Warnock, Eunice Warnock (Nichols), Mrs. Nellie Gray, Lena Gray (Adams), Mrs. Emma Bennett Winn, Kate Winn (Davis) and Mrs. Edith Roe Warnock.[1]

The first minister to serve the new church was N. H. Young, in 1902. Other early ministers were Cyrus Riffle, 1906; H. Darragh, 1909; J. G. Ragan, 1910; N. G. Griswold, 1913; W. H. Munsey, 1916; V. E. Fryman, 1920; M. A. Peters, 1922; H. J. Harvey, 1934 and O. P. Baugh, 1936. Cyrus Riffle was returned as pastor in 1911 and N. J. Griswold, 1924. When the North and South Methodist Churches united in 1939, the Fullerton Church was placed in the Ashland District with the Mount Zion Church at Frost. The first minister under the new regime was L. A. Garriot, followed by R. T. Wilson, 1941; H. S. Mastin, 1942; A. G. Allen, 1945; K. L. Harris, 1949; S. B. Rucker, 1952; J. M. Gold, 1956 and J. S. Gwinn, 1960. R. T. Wilson was returned in 1954 and died while serving this church.

In 1946 Fullerton was made a station. Plans were made to build a new church to be located at South Shore. The present brick church was erected and dedicated Easter Sunday April 16, by the

1. Names were given by Mrs. Flora Ensor.

district superintendent, Rev. Homer L. Moore, with the pastor, J. M. Gold, assisting.

Sunshine Methodist Church

REV. SAM FILLMORE

A Methodist Protestant church was organized at Sunshine March 11, 1915. E. M. Nickel and building and finance committee were elected to make arrangements and to secure money to build a church. Ground was broken and the cornerstone laid March 29, 1915, members of the church and their friends donating time and labor to build it. Dedication services were held August 29, 1915, Rev. C. H. Garrison of the Methodist Protestant Kentucky Conference preaching the dedicatory sermon.

In 1922 the church burned to the ground and a new frame church was built on the foundation. Soon after this church was damaged again by fire but was repaired and used for services. In 1948, this church was moved to the rear and the present brick church erected. Official opening services were held Sunday, January 2, 1955, the guest speaker being Dr. E. M. Fossett, who was District Superintendent of the Ashland District of the Methodist Church in Kentucky at that time. Sunshine Circuit pastors have served the Bennett Chapel, New Bethlehem and Valley Chapel Churches. In June 1958, Sunshine was made a station with Rev. Sam Fillmore pastor since that time. Rev. James A. Rayburn, who aided in the organization of the first church, was pastor 1915-1919, and again 1931-1936. Additional land for parking facilities has been donated by Mrs. Nellie Nickel Pollard.

Fraternal Orders

The following article on Freemasonry has been obtained from the best authorities. It is composed of secret societies, called lodges, which exist wherever Europeans have settled. It is founded on and professes the practice of social and moral virtues, charity and brotherly love. It possesses an elaborate ritual, numerous grades of officials, secret signs and passwords and an emblem of a circle and a square and in the center a capital G for Grand, by which members may make themselves known to each other in any part of the world. Many of these traveled far in early days whenever an important work was being built. Before the seventeenth century only brick- and stonemasons were members, but during the nineteenth century a society of masons and builders in Britain accepted some persons not belonging to the craft. Hence the name Free and Accepted Masons (F. & A.M.). This dates from London, England, where the four lodges combined.

The Greenup Masonic Lodge was the first organization of its kind in the county, having received its charter in 1827. Charter members were Thomas T. Shreve, John Trimble, Chesley Glover, John M. McConnell, Matthew Stewart, Joseph D. Collins, L. L. Shreve, John C. Kouns, Daniel Hillman, Thompson Ward, William Conner, Frederick W. Miles, Henry E. Green, Aaron Tufts, John D. Hockaday, William Smith, James D. Dunlap, Clifton A. Garrett, Benjamin F. Rankins, Cyrus Van Bibber, John B. Powell, Rowland Burns and James DeBard. The first master of the Lodge was Thomas T. Shreve. The first Masonic address was made by John M. McConnell. A Bible dated 1832, used by the lodge, was presented by John C. Kouns family. (The names of charter members were given by V. V. Kendall.)

The Greenup Eastern Star, Electra Chapter, was organized in 1895, with Charles and Lucy Sellards Taylor first Worthy Patron and Worthy Matron.

A Masonic Lodge was organized at Russell in 1895 with the following charter members: J. D. Foster, Ezra Stanley, H. A. Smith, J. A. Hill, M. R. Smith, W. D. Bernett, C. O. Honaker, C. S. Patterson, J. W. Ainsko, A G. Watkins, J. I. Bailey, H. F. Short, J. T. Cundiff, C. S. Hager, James W. Smith and J. R. Rathburn. It was named Smith Lodge. *(Russell Times)*

The Russell Eastern Star was organized in 1910, as Mistletoe Lodge, with Mrs. Addie Smith first Worthy Matron and J. D. Foster Worthy Patron.

The Russell Lodge of I.O.O.F. was organized in 1898 with twelve charter members. In 1956, O. W. Stennett served as Grandmaster of Kentucky. A lodge was organized at Greenup, in 1902, with nine charter members. A South Portsmouth Lodge was organized in 1912, with eleven charter members. The Raceland Lodge was organized in 1928 with twenty-three charter members.

Rebekah Lodges were organized at South Portsmouth in 1917 with eleven members, at Liberty, in 1921, with nineteen members and at Russell, in 1922, with seventy-seven members.

(The following was given by F. T. King):

South Portsmouth Lodge, No. 937, was established in the Christian Church at South Portsmouth by John X. Taylor, Grand Master and Fred W. Hardwick, Grand Secretary, November 17, 1930. Officers installed were G. T. Thomas, W.M.; D. E. McGlone,

S.W.; Arnold Woods, J.W.; Matthew Hanson, Secretary; Leslie May, S.D.; Turl Brooker, J.D.; and F. T. King, Tyler. Other charter members were T. P. Stone, ――― Prestwood, H. H. McDonald, Paul Jones, Ed Nichols, Kerney Hampton, Walter Craycraft, A. J. Swearingen, Seth Jones and A. W. King.

In 1942, the South Portsmouth Lodge was moved to Fullerton-South Shore. The name was changed to the Harrison-Fullerton Lodge No. 937. A new building was begun at South Shore in 1950, with the following committee, F. T. King, Chairman; Matthew Warnock, Vice Chairman; Carl Morton, Inspector; Leslie May, Treasurer; W. C. Spears, Secretary; Turl Brooker, Seth Jones and Paris Donley.

The cornerstone was laid in June, 1950. The first meeting was held in the new building March 10, 1951. The mortgage was burned September 7, 1955.

The Eastern Star Lodge was organized as Radiance Lodge in 1933 at South Portsmouth, with Mrs. F. T. King, W.M.; Turl Brooker, W.P.; F. T. King, Assistant W.P. and Mrs. Turl Brooker, Assistant W.M.

X

Wars

Revolutionary Soldiers

AT THE close of the Revolutionary War, many soldiers received grants of land in Greenup County and in their old age applied for pensions. Among those who proved their war records and were granted pensions were:

James Applegate, sergeant in First Regiment U.S. Lines.
Jeremiah Burns, private in Colonel George Matthews Virginia Co.
John Chadwick, private in North Carolina Line.
John W. Howe, private in Virginia Militia for two years.
John Johnston, private in the Connecticut Line.
James Lawson, private in Captain Moses Sutton Company in Virginia.
Elisha Mayhew was granted a pension in 1818.
James Patton, private in the Pennsylvania Line.
Charles Riggs, private in the Maryland Line.
Clayborn Sartin, private in the Virginia Line.
Godfrey Smith, private in the Virginia Line.
Andrew Zornes, private in the Pennsylvania Line.

There were other Revolutionary soldiers living in the county, who either did not apply for pensions or whose service records were missing. Among these were:

Moses Fuqua, who was a captain in the Virginia Militia.
Thomas Waring, ensign and second lieutenant in Captain Gaskin's Company, Fifty Regiment of Virginia.
William Hammon, Thomas Richards, Thomas Dixon, Thomas Hackworth, James Norton and Joseph Westlake.

Thomas Lloyd Gray took the Oath of Allegiance in Maryland and served in the Revolutionary War in Virginia. He was a private in the War of 1812. His records of the latter were missing.

John Greenslate was a private in the Revolutionary War in North Carolina. He is buried near the old homestead on Tygart Creek.

Carter Hailey was a private in the War. His service record is missing.

James Lawson enlisted as a private in Virginia. He was a soldier under General St. Clair, in 1812.

Josiah Morton was a Revolutionary soldier in Virginia, serving at the Battle of Guilford Courthouse and at the Siege of Yorktown. He came to Greenup County about 1800.

War of 1812

George Naylor Davis was a captain in the Regiment of Colonel Isaac Shelby at the Battle of the Thames. He is buried in the Brick Union Cemetery at Gray's Branch.

Moses M. Fuqua, Jr. was a private in Captain William Huston's Mounted Company from Scioto County, Ohio. He is buried on the original home farm at Mount Zion.

Samuel Wilson Gammon was stationed at Limestone (Mason County). He is buried in the Mount Zion Cemetery.

Thomas Lloyd Gray—service record missing.

Major James Howe served as a private at the Battle of New Orleans. He is probably buried at Oldtown, where he lived.

John C. Kouns was major of the First Kentucky Regiment and was on the staff of General Andrew Jackson at the Battle of New Orleans. He is buried in the Greenup Cemetery.

James Lawson enlisted in Captain Robert Loman's Company in Virginia. He served with General Arthur St. Clair in the northwest and in the War of 1812. Place of burial not known but, probably is in Mount Zion Cemetery.

Civil War

Joshua Bailey served as a private in Company I, Tenth Kentucky Cavalry.

Charles and Thomas Bailey served as privates, the latter in the Twenty-second Kentucky Regiment.

George M. Baker served two years as a private in Company K, Fortieth Kentucky Infantry.

James W. Burton served as a private one year in Company K, Tenth Kentucky Cavalry.

John W. Burton served one year in Company F, Fifty-fourth Kentucky Cavalry (Mounted).

Thomas Burton served in the Fifty-fourth Kentucky Infantry.

James Carr served in Company C, Twenty-second Kentucky Infantry.

Henry Colegrove served in Company B, Twenty-second Kentucky Infantry.

Henry Diedrich was a private in Company K, Tenth Kentucky Cavalry.

James W. Greenslate enlisted in Company A, Forty-fifth Kentucky Infantry.

Captain Carter Hailey enlisted in Company D, Thirty-ninth Kentucky Infantry. He was promoted to lieutenant and commissioned Captain of the Regiment. His father, Carter Hailey, served in the War of 1812 and a son, Alfred, was also a soldier in the Civil War.

George Kaut was a private in Company K, Fifty-third Mounted Infantry.

John Moran joined Company F, Fifty-fourth Kentucky Mounted Infantry. He was postmaster 1872-1882.

Shadrach Lindsay Mitchell joined Company C, Twenty-second Regiment Kentucky Infantry. He served three years as first sergeant and lieutenant.

John James Tanner enlisted in the Confederate Army, Company C, Second Battalion, Kentucky Mounted Rifles. He was buried in the family cemetery near Little Sandy Falls and, at the death of his wife at Henderson, his body was taken there.

Francis Coburn Robb joined the Twenty-second Regiment of Kentucky Volunteer Militia. He was commissioned first lieutenant.

John H. Willis joined Company E, Fifth Regiment, West Virginia Volunteer Infantry. He is buried with his wife in the Christian Church Cemetery at Siloam, Kentucky.

William Jackson Worthington was captain of Company B, Twenty-second Kentucky Volunteer Infantry, and was promoted to the rank of colonel.

Charles Brooker served in the Civil War and was the last living soldier in the county, dying at Beattyville at the age of ninety-five years.

Pleasant Timberlake was a private in the Civil War. His record is missing.

Spanish-American War—1898

Sixty-nine soldiers were enrolled at Greenup, under Captain George A. Corum, in Company B, Fourth Kentucky Regiment. They were mustered in at Lexington July 6, 1898, and mustered out February 12, 1899, at Anniston, Alabama. A list of names is contained in *A History of Greenup County*.

Vernon, son of Henry and Electa McGinness Taylor of Tygart, was killed in the Spanish-American War. His name is not listed with Captain George A. Corum's Regiment, as he enlisted at Ashland, Kentucky.

War Casualties

James, son of Gabriel and Mary Stark Anglin of the southeastern section of the county, was killed in the Civil War.

Travis Collard, son of Rev. Allan and Elizabeth Brown Kendall, was born in Morgan County in 1840. He married Virginia Anglin. He was a soldier in the Civil War and was killed at Sandy Hook, Kentucky, in 1864. He is buried at Sandy Hook.

Henry M. Rust was a member of the state senate, 1857-1861. He enlisted in the Civil War in the Big Sandy area. He was wounded in the Battle of Ivy Mountain, November 8, 1861, and died shortly after. His body was returned to Greenup County for burial.

Vernon, son of Henry and Electa McGinness Taylor, of Tygart Valley, was killed in the Spanish-American War of 1898.

Malcolm, son of Emmett and Myrtle Spence Norris, was lost when the submarine *Gudgeon* disappeared during World War I.

World War II

James Robb, son of James Robb and Rebecca Morton Sowards, was born December 25, 1923, in Greenup, Kentucky. He graduated from the Greenup High School and from Ashland Junior College. He was a member of the Christian Church of Greenup.

He enlisted in the United States Army in May, 1943, and received training in Texas, at Syracuse University, in Mississippi, and at Fort Benning, Georgia. He was sent to the European Theater in the 101st Airborne Division and was a paratrooper in the Battle of Bastogne, Belgium, where he was killed in the performance of duty. He was buried at Bastogne with the five thousand men who lost their lives there. His body was later returned to Greenup County for burial.

Charles Brooks Kendall, son of Vernon V. and Mary Norris Kendall, was born March 6, 1924, in Greenup, Kentucky. He graduated from Greenup Grade and Ashland Senior High School where he was a member of the R.O.T.C. He was an active member of the Boy Scouts and attained the rank of Eagle Scout at the age of fifteen years.

He enlisted in the United States Naval Reserves June 17, 1943, and was sent to the Naval Air Technical Center at Navy Pier, Chicago, Illinois, for training. He also received training at Memphis, Tennessee, at Jacksonville, Florida, Banana River, Florida, Corpus Christi, Texas, and at San Diego, California. He, with nine others, received high praise from their commanding officer upon completion of study and demonstration of marksmanship with aerial weapons. With the rank of AMMF, 2nd Class, he was flight engineer and plane captain on a Martin Mariner, a Navy patrol bomber. He left the United States on February 25, 1945, from San Diego, for Kaneche Bay, Hawaii, and then to John Island, Ebeye, Saipan and Okinawa, where in the faithful performance of duty September 12, 1945, just off the coast of Okinawa, Charles with members of his crew, died for his country. His plane crashed in midair with the amphibian Navy Plane J2F.

Charles was twenty-one years and six months old. He was buried with military honors September 13, 1945, in the Island Command Cemetery on Okinawa. His parents received his body February 8, 1950, and burial was made in the Bellefont Memorial Park Cemetery with graveside service conducted by Howard Thomas Post, American Legion.

Korean War

Andrew Wayne, twin son of Andrew Wayne and Olive Fannin King, was born December 24, 1932, in the Mount Zion community of Greenup County. Later they moved to Portsmouth, Ohio, where the twins attended grade school and two years of high school. In 1949, Andrew Wayne, Sr., was promoted by his company (N & W RR) to Roanoke, Virginia, where the twins graduated from Jefferson High School.

Andrew Wayne King, Jr., enlisted in the 508th Airborne Division of Paratroopers, ABD Pat, Roanoke, in February, 1951. He received training at Fort Jackson and Fort Benning, Georgia, and as sergeant first class, Company D, Seventeenth Regiment (Infantry) he was sent to Korea, October, 1952. A telegram dated

July 19, 1953, reported him missing in action since July 9th after the Battle of Pork Chop Hill. James Alfred enlisted a few months after his twin at Roanoke, followed step by step in his brother's path and reached Korea to join him on July 12, 1953 only to learn that he had been reported missing three days before. He was forward observer on the farthest outpost on Pork Chop Hill. A version given by a companion observer who escaped from the overwhelming force of artillery and grenades is that, when he looked back from the bottom of the hill, he saw "Jack" surrounded by Chinese Reds. All that could be done by the chaplain and "Jim" failed, and no trace of him has ever been found.

American Legion

Two American Legion posts have been organized in Greenup County. Howard Thomas Post No. 43 was organized at Russell at the close of World War I. It was named in honor of the first to lose his life in that war.

The James L. Flannery Post No. 276 was organized at Fullerton-South Shore at the close of World War II. It was named in honor of James L. Flannery, the first in this area to lose his life in that war. The purpose of the American Legion is to promote Americanism and patriotism and to preserve the memories of the comrades of all wars.

XI

Families

FROM W. F. BLACK, of Georgetown, Kentucky, we have received the following concerning the Andrew Hood family, of which Mr. Black is a descendant. Major Andrew Hood was born in Frederick County, Virginia, in 1745. He was a son of Lucas and Joanna Hood. He married Massa Suddith in Virginia before 1770 and came to Kentucky in 1785. His name has been found in the tax lists of Bourbon, Clark and Mason Counties. Andrew, Jr., married Mary Kane in Greenup County in 1807.

From Marvin C. Nichols of Fort Worth, Texas, we have the following information. Nicholas, a son of John and Cassandra Wilcoxen Nichols, married Eliza Slater in 1826, supposedly in Greenup County. Their children were Thomas, James, Isaac, William, Harrison, Esther and Sallie.

The following information concerning the Chinn family shows that Benjamin Chinn married Nancy Nichols in Greenup County February 20, 180?. Their children were John, Lewis, George, Alfred and Christopher. Nancy married James Harvey, and Cassandra married Thomas B. King in 1841, and after his death married Obadiah Mackoy; Alfred, the fourth son of Benjamin and Nancy Nichols Chinn, married Judith Mackoy and went to Missouri to live. He was killed in the Civil War and Judith returned with her children to her father's home near Siloam. She later moved to Illinois with her children, John, Richard and Florence. Descendants of this family living in Illinois visited the old unoccupied Obadiah Mackoy homestead.

When Samuel, the pioneer of the Walker family, died, he was buried on his farm at Walker's Landing. After twenty-one years, his body was removed to the Mount Zion Churchyard, where he and his wife lie buried under a stone crypt on which is engraved, "Samuel Walker died January 4, 1832, aged 69 years," on one side, and on the other, "Ann, consort of Samuel Walker, died December 20, 1841."

In the Virgin family history of *A History of Greenup County*, the name of Harvey was unintentionally omitted. He married Rebecca Brown of Oldtown, and their children were Bertha (Mrs. William Floyd), Ollie (Mrs. Wilford Vicars), Grover, May (Mrs. Leonard Montgomery), Elwood, Denver, Edward and Homer. Grover married Elizabeth Barker, Elwood married Mary Cameron, Denver married June Floyd, Edward married Annie Potter, and Homer married Capitola Barber.

Anderson (W. Tong West)

The parents of James Anderson, who settled in the western part of the county at an early date, had emigrated from Scotland to Pennsylvania. James (1792-1882) was born in the United States. He married Helica Dortch, whose family had also come from Pennsylvania. The Anderson farm was at the intersection of the Shultz and White Oak roads. James and Helica Anderson died the same day and were buried in the same grave in the Anderson Cemetery on Flat Hollow.

James and Helica Dortch Anderson were the parents of twelve children: Wesley (1817-1878), Noah (1818) who married Huldah Abbott, William (1821-1880) who married (1) —— Jones and (2) Elizabeth Hicks, James (1823) who went West and was never heard from, Mary (1828) who married David Turner, Richard (1831-1863) who died in California, Jacob (1833-1892) who married Martha Jane Dunaway, Matthias (1835) who married Mollie Christy, Jesse (1838) who married (1) —— Smith and (2) Martha Johnson, Lucinda, twin of Jesse married John Whitman and died in 1882, Thomas (1840-1869), and Elijah (1843) who married Phoebe Stafford.

James Anderson served in the War of 1812 and five of his sons, Wesley, Noah, William, Matthias and Jesse, served in the Union Army. Jacob, the seventh son, married Martha Jane, daughter of James P. and Rachel McQuillen Dunaway. Their five children were Ella, Emma, Low, Fidelia and Myrtle, all of whom, except Low who died in California, are buried in the Mount Zion Churchyard. James P. Dunaway kept a general store at the foot of Springville Hill for many years. The three children of the family were Isaac, a physician, James and Martha Jane (1845-1896).

Emma, daughter of Jacob and Martha Jane Anderson, married James W. West of Limeville, where they made their home. They were the parents of two sons, William Tong and Charles. Tong married Doris Ruth Zimmerman, of Portland, Oregon. They are the parents of three sons, Dan, David and Ralph. Charles married Edith Craft, and their children are Charles, Rita Ensor, James and John. Both families have their homes on the original Tong land at Limeville.

Berkeley (Dorothy Berkeley Moore)

The Berkeley family originated in England, emigrating to America in early colonial days, settling in Virginia, starting with the family of William Berkeley.

Thomas Berkeley, born in 1790 and died in 1871, was the son of William Berkeley II, and grandson of William Berkeley I, who were all wealthy planters and slaveholders until the time of the rebellion, when their estate dwindled. Thomas Berkeley grew up in Fairfax, Virginia, leaving there and going to the Shenandoah Valley in 1818. He enlisted in the War of 1812, was commissioned first lieutenant, and raised a company in the Valley of Virginia. He lost all his possessions while in the Shenandoah Valley, and he moved from there to Greenup County, Kentucky, in 1822, settling across the river from Haverhill, Ohio.

Thomas Berkeley's son James Herman Berkeley married Elizabeth Ann Davidson, daughter of Judge Nathaniel Davidson of Ironton, Ohio, and their son James Marshall Berkeley married Elizabeth Collins, daughter of James Collins on March 19, 1877, and this same year they settled on a farm four miles from Greenup on Little Sandy River. To them were born four sons: Homer Herman, William Allen, Benjamin Cleveland and Clarence Leslie (all are now deceased). They grew up and spent most of their lives on their father's farm. Today this farm is in the possession of the family of Clarence Leslie Berkeley.

Some years after 1812, some of the members of the Berkeley families, realizing that they bore the same name as Governor William Berkeley of colonial days, decided to change their name, spelling it thus: Berkley, Burkley, Barkley, Buckley, Beckley.

Brooker (Turl Brooker)

Jacob Brooker (German Brucker) came from Germany to America early in 1800. He had been a soldier in Napoleon's army. A great-grandson, Turl Brooker of South Portsmouth, has a paper in excellent condition, printed in German, giving the enlistment of Jacob Brucker at Grosherzog, in 1813, and his discharge at Mannheim, in 1818.

Jacob Brooker I settled in Ohio, probably near Massilon. His son, Jacob II, served in the Mexican War. Jacob III was a soldier in the Civil War, having enlisted in Company A, Fifth Regiment Infantry, in 1861, in West Virginia. He re-enlisted in the same company in 1863. He died in the town of Beattyville, west of Springville (South Portsmouth), and is buried with the soldiers in Greenlawn Cemetery, Portsmouth, Ohio.

Jacob Brooker II married Lizzie Gibson, probably at Massillon, Ohio, where the family lived at the time. Turl, son of Jacob III, married Rose Williams of Springville. A son, Raymond Jacob, married Helen Reeder of South Portsmouth, is a teacher and lives west of South Portsmouth. Harry, another son of Jacob III, married Nancy Hanners of South Portsmouth. Their children are Ralph, who married Mary Emma May of South Portsmouth, John, who married Helen Lamblin and lives in Columbus, and a daughter Ruth.

Corum (George Corum)

The Jesse Corum family came from Pennsylvania to Greenupsburg in early 1800. He was made a justice in 1820 and was elected to the Kentucky legislature in 1844. The children of the family were William, Jesse, Eliza Ann, Amanda K., Rebecca, America and Margaret. William married Edith Pallmore, whose family had come from Pennsylvania, and they were the parents of George Alexander, Mary and Sallie. He was elected county clerk in 1836 and served until 1876. His son, George A., was elected in 1876 and served until 1908. He married Lena Taft, and their children are Edith, Mary Oney, George and Taft, who is married and living at Dayton, Ohio. Mary married James McCormick of Ohio, and Sallie went West to visit relatives and remained there.

Jesse Corum II married Sarah Stewart, June 15, 1855. They were the parents of Maud, Laura, Kate, Lily and Earnest (?). Several of these moved West. Mrs. Jesse Corum married Charles F. Mytinger and later joined the children. Ann Eliza married Jeremiah Davidson, Amanda, Charles Raisin, and went West. Rebecca married Edwin Heisler, America, Ayak N. Triplett and Margaret, James L. Stewart. Of these, the Davidson and Heisler families remained in Greenup.

Eifort

Col. Sebastian Eifort was born near Frankfort, Germany, in 1817. He came with his parents to America in 1832. They settled at Lancaster, Pennsylvania. He went to Jackson, Ohio, in 1836, and was later connected with the iron furnace there. He married Rachel, daughter of William and Rachel Tomlinson Jackson. He became manager of Bloom Furnace in Scioto County and helped to build and operate Harrison Furnace.

In 1855, Sebastian Eifort and his family moved to Kentucky. He bought land in Carter County and helped to build Boone Furnace, which was operated later under the name of Eifort, Bennett and Company. In 1869, he sold his interest in Boone Furnace and became manager of Hunnewell Furnace, where he remained for thirteen years. He retired to his home on Main Street, in Greenup, where he died in 1893.

On March 17, 1892, Col. Eifort and his wife celebrated their golden wedding anniversary at their home in Greenup. An interesting incident was that Aunt Evaline Jackson (colored) who had prepared the wedding supper for Mamie, the youngest daughter, twenty-two years before, was the presiding cook at the anniversary celebration for the parents.

Col. and Mrs. Eifort were the parents of nine children, William Henry, James M., Kate, Mary Jane, Fabian S., Joseph B., Warren, Charles and Oscar. William Henry served in the Civil War with ranks of captain, major and lieutenant colonel. He was killed at Tricene, Tennessee, in 1864, and is buried in Greenlawn Cemetery at Portsmouth, Ohio. Kate married John Warnock, agent for Boone Furnace and later mail agent for E.K.R.R. Mr. Warnock died but the family, Myra, Annie, Ray and Henry, lived in Greenup for many years. Annie married Nathaniel Callon and Ray married Nellie Scott before the family moved to Califorina. The second daughter of Col. and Mrs. Eifort, Mary Jane (Mamie), married Charles Hertel, a merchant of Greenup. They were the parents of Laura Baldwin of St. Albans, W. Va., Nora, who married Robert L. Wilson, Rachel, who married Marvin Miller, William E. (Brownie), and Clifford, who married Martha Crawford and lived at Hinton, W. Va. Fabian married Margaret Alexander and was in business with his father at Hunnewell Furnace, living for some time in the Eifort home at Greenup. Children of the family were Nell, Harry E., Louis C., Ina and Hazel.

The family moved to Ashland, where members of the family are still living. Joseph married Agnes Radspinner. They moved to North Carolina.

Floyd (Jarvey Floyd)

Floyd, an English name, was originally Lloyd and has an interesting history of how it came into existence. The Lloyd family split because of a disagreement over giving the common people a voice in the control of the government and liberalizing insurance and finance to cover the peasants, or common people. This resulted in the banishment of the Lloyds favoring such a move and of the dropping of the first L, substituting F, meanings Friends of the common people.

Two members of the Floyd family came to America with the early English settlers, because of persecution as Separatists in the mother country. This, with reports of fertile soil, rich timberlands and opportunities for freedom and independence that were sent back to relatives, encouraged Thomas Floyd and his friend David Colley, a Baptist minister, to come to Virginia and from there to Kentucky where they surveyed and homesteaded fifteen hundred acres on Upper Crane Creek in Greenup County.

Hick Floyd, father of Thomas, came from the old salt works of Washington County, Virginia, and established a home on Crane Creek, below which the Primitive Baptist Church stands. The present church (1928) is a continuation of that established by Elder David Colley when he came to Crane Creek. The Hick Floyd family consisted of Dave, William, Thomas, Hick, Jr., Martha, Sarah, Lizzie and Nellie. Dave married Mary J. Stewart and their children were Thomas J., William O., David C., Lee, Betty and Mary. Thomas J. married Emma Moore, William O. married Margaret Bush, David married Sallie A. Smith, Lee married Watt Montgomery, Betty married Alonzo Alexander, and Mary married Porter Gilbert. Children of Thomas J. and Emma Floyd were Dee, Ellis, Porter, Joe, Roy, Nellie, Anna and Leona. William O. and Margaret Bush Floyd were parents of William, Charles, Ottie (the mother of Roscoe Stephens, superintendent of schools), Ida R., Anglin and Betty Riffe. David and Sallie A. Smith Floyd were the parents of Jarvey, Winfield, Talton D., Smith, James W., Mary L., Julie, Nola, Frances T., Hazel I., Effie and Virginia. Children of Lee Floyd and Watt Montgomery were John, who lives on on original survey, Thomas D., Dove and Lucille. Betty Floyd and Alonzo Alexander were the parents of Cephas, Charles, Floyd, Grace, Mary, Augusta, Sallie and Fern. Mary L. Floyd and Porter Gilbert were the parents of Lillard, Floyd, Oliver, Earl, Lorena and Evalina. Of these, Roscoe Stephens established a home near Maloneton. Jarvey is at present clerk and civil service examiner with the Post Office at Portsmouth, Ohio. He married Mary Hazel Tankersly. They reside at New Boston, Ohio. Mrs. Floyd is, at present, Deputy State Counsellor D. of A. Lodge and Welfare Director.

In early days the Floyd families were engaged in hauling ore and charcoal to the iron furnaces, and in shipping tanbark, bridge and ship timbers, staves to the cooperage at Greenup and telephone poles later, by way of the E.K.R.R. (Kinkead's *History of Kentucky* contains much history of John Floyd who came to Kentucky as a surveyor of Fincastle County in 1776 and was also a member of the first court at Harrodsburg in 1777. Floyd County, Kentucky, was named in honor of John B. Floyd, Secretary of War in 1857.)

Smith (Jarvey Floyd)

Francis Marion and Mary Claxton Smith (see *A History of Greenup County*) came from Owen County, Kentucky, in 1888 to Crane Creek and bought one thousand acres. He was a large tobacco grower and buyer, shipping tobacco in hogsheads to the Farmer's Tobacco Warehouse at Louisville, Kentucky, by way of the E.K.R.R. Mr. Smith died at his home on Crane Creek in 1921. Mrs. Smith celebrated her one hundredth birthday March 11, 1949. Mr. and Mrs. Smith were the parents of twelve children, ten of them living at the time of her death in 1950.

Garrett (Leslie Gardner)

(The following history of the Garrett family was sent to the author by Leslie Gardner of New York City.)

There were thirteen Garretts that came from England to Virginia from 1607-1716. William Garrett came to Jamestown in 1607. He was a bricklayer and was mentioned (as William Garrit) in Captain John Smith's list of early settlers. In 1620, William Garrett was present at a meeting of the Virginia Company in London, and was described as an inhabitant of Virginia for thirteen years.

A William Garrett, born in Virginia between 1710 and 1715, married Elizabeth Ashton, and two sons were William and John. Deeds for William and his wife Elizabeth are on record in Spottsylvania, Louisa, Albemarle and other counties. A will of William Garrett dated May 8, 1780, and filed June 12, 1780, in Louisa County, Virginia, leaves "to my wife Elizabeth, plantation, Negroes, stock and household furniture for life; to my son William land on Cranks Run & etc.; to my son Henry land in Spottsylvania and etc. At the death of my wife everything is to be divided equally among all of my children, William, Henry, Ann Johnson, Elizabeth Terrill and Susanna Johnson, Executors William and Henry Garrett.

Captain Henry Garrett (1745-1815) married 1765 Mary Johnson of Louisa County. Among their thirteen children were Thomas, Henry, William, Mary, Elizabeth and Richard. In 1810, Captain Henry Garrett moved to Lexington in Fayette County, Kentucky. He had been Clerk of the Committee of Safety of Louisa County, Virginia, in 1775, formed by the First Continental Congress, at Philadelphia, October 20, 1774. He was a private in Captain John Blackwell's Company No. 4, in 1778, and was sworn in as captain in 1781. He fought at the Battle of Yorktown and witnessed the surrender of Cornwallis. He was made sheriff of Louisa County, Virginia, August 12, 1800.

Thomas Johnson, oldest son of Captain Henry and Mary Johnson Garrett, was born 1777, probably in Louisa County, Virginia, and died 1855. He married (1) Lucinda Terrill (who died leaving a young son, Murdock, who remained with his grandfather when Thomas came to Lexington, Kentucky) and (2) Nancy Thomson. From Lexington, Thomas and Nancy moved to Mount Sterling, where he built the first ropewalk. In his later life he moved to Coal Branch, Greenup County. Their children were Clifton A. George, Alexander, Sophia, Moriah, Sally Ann and Catherine. Clifton and George were deputy sheriffs under Thomas B. King, 1827-1829. Catherine, born at Lexington, Kentucky, married Robert Scott (at Grayson, Kentucky) and lived at the furnaces: Ohio and Mount Vernon in Lawrence County and at Laurel Furnace in Greenup County (see Scott family in *A History of Greenup County*).

Clifton A. married Sarah M. King November 8, 1824, with Thomas B. King, bondsman. Their daughter Martha Ann married Richard Morton (see Morton Family in *A History of Greenup County*).

Hertel (Mrs. Frances Corum)

George F. Hertel was an early settler of Greenupsburg. He was a shoemaker and had his shop on Washington between Main and Elizabeth Streets. In 1864, this building was bought by Benjamin F. Pratt, who with Thomas Brooks erected the building where they conducted the general store of Pratt and Brooks. This building, still in good condition, houses the business of Harley Van Hoose.

Charles, a son of George F. Hertel, married Mamie, a daughter of Mr. and Mrs. Sebastian Eifort (see Eifort). In the 1870's and 1880's Mr. Hertel conducted a general store in the present building at Main and Laurel Street. During these years the Hertel home stood on the present site of the Shepherd-McCubbin Garage, and he later purchased a home at Main and Hickory Street.

Children of Mr. and Mrs. Hertel were Laura Baldwin, of St. Albans, West Virginia; William, who died in boyhood; Nora, who married Robert L. Wilson; Rachel Miller, of Circleville, Ohio; and Clifford, who resides at Hinton, West Virginia. Frances, a daughter of Robert L. and Nora Hertel Wilson, married George, a son of George and Lena Taft Corum, and resides in East Greenup.

Jones (W. Leslie Myers)

Rival Doolittle Jones was born August 22, 1796. He was a son of Griffith Jones and wife, who came from Maryland to Mason County, Kentucky, and was a neighbor of Samuel Glover, who came from Maryland about the same time (1796). Both families settled near Mays Lick and may have been related. In 1800, Elijah, son of Samuel, married Catherine, daughter of Griffith Jones, and in 1804 moved to Alexandria at the mouth of the Scioto River and later to Portsmouth where he lived until he died. Rival, a son of Griffith Jones, married Mary M. Fuqua, a daughter of William and Sarah Morton Fuqua, September 29, 1821, and settled on a large farm at Lynn, in Greenup County. Rival D. and Mary Fuqua Jones were the parents of Oratio Nelson, Samuel, William, Mary, Louise and Maria. Of these, Oratio N. and Martha Moseley Jones were the only members of the family to make their home in Greenup County. Samuel married Mary Lyon May 13, 1859. They went to Ohio, and at Galena operated a tannery built by the father of U. S. Grant. William married a Miss Powers, and they were the parents of two daughters, Pauline and Stella. They lived at Esculapia Springs in Lewis County and operated the hotel there, a popular summer resort for many years. Mary married Samuel Bell Pugh of Lynn. They moved to Vanceburg where the Pugh store was an institution for many years. Maria and Louise, unmarried, lived on the Jones farm at Esculapia. Rival and Mary Fuqua Jones went to Lewis County where they died and are buried.

[103]

Oratio Nelson and Martha Moseley Jones were the parents of Malcolm, Rufus, Lon, Robert and Nellie. Malcolm married Sallie Crossett of Smith Branch. They were the parents of William, who was killed in a railroad accident at Covington, Kentucky, when a young man; Ora; Charles; and Lucy (Dolly), Malcolm and Sallie Crossett lived for many years on a farm near Lynn, Kentucky, Malcolm, Rufus, Lon, Robert and Nettie. Malcolm married Sallie moving later to Alabama. Rufus and Lon and the daughter Nettie went to Lewis County where they married and established their homes. Robert married Edna, daughter of Dr. and Mrs. Charles Secrest, of Lynn, where they resided for several years and where their sons Eugene and Vernon were born. Eugene died in boyhood and Vernon became a physician and practiced at Dayton, Kentucky. Mr. and Mrs. Robert Jones had moved from Lynn to Covington, Kentucky. Nettie taught school in Lewis County. She married Leslie Myers and they were the parents of W. Leslie Myers, of Lewis and Mason Counties.

Lawson

Thomas Lawson (1779) married (probably in Portsmouth as the William Lawson family had settled in Scioto County) Barbara Earson, a relative of the family of which William had married a member, Susannah Earson. They settled in Kentucky, across the river from Munn's Run, owning the farm that was bought by Benjamin F. King, Jr., in 1883, who lived in the old house until he built the large brick house (in 1885) on the knoll below it. While leveling land for a tenant house, several gravestones were uncovered, one of which bore the name of Barbara Lawson. Children of Thomas and Barbara Earson Lawson were Silas, Ben F., James N., John, William, Jacob and Mary Parker.

After the death of Barbara, Thomas Lawson married Ada Horn. A will of Thomas Lawson dated May 4, 1842, reads: "to my sons Silas, Ben F. and James N. . . . and to my son John one half of my land on lower side of Tygart Creek, including the part I gave my son, William (died) which shall be divided between him and my son Jacob, John to have the upper part. I, also, give to my two sons, John and Jacob the land I own on the east or upper side of Tygart." A daughter, Mary Parker and his second wife, Ada Horn Lawson were given land on the Ohio River and "to my stepson Jonathan Horn the sum of $100 when he shall come of age. Executors are my son Silas and Thomas B. King."

A William Lawson Inventory dated February 16, 1835, was attested by Benjamin F. King, Thomas B. King and James Walker.

Montgomery (Leonard Montgomery)

The Montgomery family came to Greenup County from Virginia at an early date of the 1800's. Early records show that a marriage license was issued to John Montgomery and Mary J. Howe March 13, 1835, by permit of James Howe, parent, and that James Montgomery and Martha Brown were married November 27, 1835, with Daniel Howe bondsman. A descendant, James Montgomery, married Lucretia Belle Norris and made a home at Oldtown near the old Montgomery and Howe farms.

Daniel, a son of James and Lucretia Belle Norris Montgomery, married Ellen Davisson and settled on Crane Creek. Children of the family were Leander, Joseph, Mary, Nannie, Watt and Mrs. Thomas Kouns. Leander married Laura Belle Riffe, and they were the parents of Carrie, Leonard, Eula, Julia, May, Beckham, Charline, Lawrence and Orville.

Leonard married (1) Carrie Floyd and their children were William L., Lucille Deemer, Alene Booton, and Gretchen Stanley. Mr. Montgomery married (2) May, a daughter of Elza and Rebecca Brown Virgin, of Oldtown, Kentucky. Mr. Montgomery is a merchant at King's Addition.

Moseley (Cabell)

The Moseley family was listed in England at the time of the Norman Conquest (1066) and the hamlet of Moseley, or Mosleii, as it is in the Domesday Book, a survey made for William the Conqueror (1086), was leased by one Ernald, a common Moseley ancestor. From Ernold the descent went through Oswald de Moseley of Ancoats (see *Virginia Magazine*, vols. 31-32-33, and the Shires of Cheshire and Lancaster for description and verification of Coat of Arms and Motto: *Moslegem regit*—or, *regis*).

From Oswald the descent came through Jenkyn, who in 1465 lived at Hough End. Jenkyn's son, James, succeeded him, and James was succeeded by his son Edward, who died in 1511, leaving three sons, Oswald, Nicholas and Anthony. Oswald was the ancestor of William, the Emigrant. Oswald's son William was a prosperous cloth merchant on trade between England and Holland. He married Dorothy Helms of Oxfordshire. Three sons were Richard, Charles and William. Their father, Oswald, died in 1642. William came to Lower Norfolk County, Virginia, in 1649 with his wife, Susanna Crokroft, and two sons, Arthur and William. He was elected Commissioner of Justice in Lower Norfolk County (now Princess Anne) which administered all affairs of the county.

Nicholas, who was Lord Mayor of London in 1599, and his brother Anthony, dropped the letter "e" from their name. William, the Emigrant, died in 1655 and in his will left his property to be equally divided among his wife and two sons Arthur and William. William married Mary Gookin and lived a prominent and useful citizen in Lower Norfolk. The Colonial Vestry Book records names of his descendants serving on the Vestry. Arthur Moseley married Susan Hancock. He was active in both State and Church affairs and was a Burgess of Lower Norfolk County in 1676. Children of Arthur and Susan Hancock Moseley were Susanna, Mary, William and Edward. By his second marriage to Ann Hargrove, he had Benjamin, Arthur, George and Amos. Arthur married Sarah Hancock in 1673 and lived in Henrico County, Virginia. Their son, Arthur, married the widow of Thomas Jamis(t)on. Two of their six sons, Arthur and John, went to Bedford County and bought land. In 1772, John sold his land to Arthur and returned to his home in Cumberland County.

Arthur was a man of affairs in Bedford County, Virginia, holding many important offices. In 1779 he served as second lieutenant in the Revolutionary Army and was sheriff of the county when he died in 1803. He married Nancy Trigg of Bedford County in 1777. They had two sons, Bennett Williamson (1780), and John. Bennett Williamson was educated as a physician and received his diploma from the Pennsylvania College of Medicine in Philadelphia. He married Elizabeth Winston in 1801. A son, George Cabell Moseley (1808), married Mary Daniel Whitlock (1815) in 1835. Their son, William Henry Moseley (1844), married Catherine Turner (1843) in 1868. A son Cabell Moseley (1873), married, in 1903, Araminta Brown of Mount Hope, W. Va. They had two daughters, Martha Moseley Taylor of Monongahela, Pennsylvania, and Mary Inez, who married Richard Dupuy. They have two daughters, Araminta and Elizabeth Jayne.

(Note: The above complete history of the Cabell Moseley family was given by Mrs. Inez Moseley Dupuy.)

Moseley (Daniel)

William Moseley, the Emigrant, came from England to Virginia between 1642 and 1650. A descendant, Daniel Perow Moseley, was born in Buckingham County, Virginia, June 22, 1783. When he was about thirteen years old, he came with his parents to Fayette County, Kentucky. About 1800, the family went to Montgomery County, near Mount Sterling. August 26, 1813, he enlisted in Richard Menefee's Company of Kentucky Militia and was made lieutenant. With his cousins Peter G. and Creed Glover, first and second sergeants, he participated in the Battle of the Thames, in Canada. In 1802, he married Mildred, a daughter of Thomas Jamison, who had emigrated from Culpeper County, Virginia, in 1782.

Daniel taught school and preached in churches of the Christian denomination in northern and central Kentucky. He studied law and practiced in Greenup County. He settled on a farm, near Lynn, on Tygart Creek. Daniel and Mildred Jamison Moseley were the parents of nine children, of whom George was appointed Adjutant General of Ohio by Governor Bartley. A daughter, Martha, married Oratio Nelson Jones, the oldest son of Rival and Mary Fuqua Jones, April 20, 1844. They lived on the Daniel and Mildred Moseley farm near Lynn and were charter members of the Liberty Christian Church in 1850. Daniel was probably its first minister and O. N. Jones, who had married his daughter Martha, was minister of the church for more than thirty years. Rival Jones was the original owner of the farm at Lynn bought by Cabell Moseley in 1910. It had become the property of the Edward Brooks family. (The two Moseley families, Cabell and Daniel, came from Virginia and settled near Lynn, not many miles apart, the Daniel Moseley family in the 1820's and the Cabell Moseleys in 1910, yet had never known each other.)

(Note: The above history was given by Mrs. Leslie Myers of Lewis County, whose mother was Nettie, daughter of O.N. and Martha Moseley Jones. A marriage record connected with this family reads, "Thomas Moseley and Martha Horn were married in Greenup County April 4, 1834, with consent of Frederick Horn.")

Mosley (William Robert Mosley)

William Mosley came from England to Virginia and may be William the Emigrant named in other Moseley ancestry, who came to Virginia in 1649. One William Mosley of Virginia had children named Samuel, James, Henderson, Richard, Ann and Armina. Samuel came from Virginia and settled in Lawrence County, Kentucky. The children were Susan, Martha, George, Rebecca, Nancy and William Robert, the last named being born in Lawrence

County. Richard Mosley emigrated to Arkansas. William Robert Mosley came to Greenup County in 1911. He married Miss Nora Mowery. He was ordained a Baptist minister in 1932 and was pastor of one charge for fourteen years. Mr. Mosley and his wife had no children but adopted a boy and a girl, whom they reared to adulthood.

Nichols (Mrs. Gertrude Nichols Hammond)

Gilbert Nichols married Martha, a daughter of Ellis Taylor and his second wife, Caroline Stuart. They were the parents of thirteen children: Ellis, John, James Gilbert, Julia Tackett, Aura Cremeans, Laura Wadkins, Berdilla Bentley, Nellie Bentley, Nettie Johnson, Lilly Davis, Martha Bradley, Edith Curry and Nancy Moore. Members of these families reside not far from the original Tygart home.

Dr. Ellis Nichols was a practicing physician at Fullerton where he died. He married Milly Holbrook and they were the parents of a daughter, Nettie, who is married and living in Washington, D.C., where her mother also resides. John married Gertrude, a daughter of William and Hannah Meenach Gray of Tygart Valley. They are the parents of Winnie, at home, Bernice Newsome, Gertrude Hammond, Wayne and Wade.

Early marriage dates of the Tygart families are:

Susan Nichols and Cornelius Meeks, Jan. 9, 1827
Adeline Nichols and Mark Roberts, Feb. 10, 1834
Rachel Nichols and Jacob Barney, Nov. 12, 1840

Scott (Leslie Gardner)

(Additional history of the Scott family, was received from Lester D. Gardner of New York City, a relative of the family, too late to include in *A History of Greenup County*.)

The Scott family came from Scotland via Ireland to Pennsylvania about the middle of 1770 and from there down the Ohio River about 1785. David and Nancy Welsh Scott settled in Harrison County, near Cynthiana. A son, Thomas, born in Leesburg, Kentucky, moved to Grayson and bought land on the Little Sandy River. He was a salt maker, tanner, farmer and owner of the Pactolus Iron Furnace. He built the first brick house within the present limits of Carter County. He died in 1871 and his will, recorded at Grayson, names as heirs his sons A.J., Henry and Robert, and daughters Delilah Thompson and Eliza A. Frizzell, also a grandson, William Kibby, son of a daughter Mary.

A son, Henry, was born in 1808 at Leesburg, Kentucky. He married Catherine Garrett and died in 1890. He was in the furnace business at Pactolus and lived in Grayson until 1850 when he became interested in Ohio and Mount Vernon furnaces in Lawrence County, Ohio. He bought Laurel Furnace in Greenup County in the early 1860's and when furnace days were coming to an end in the 1870's the family went to Ironton where Mr. Scott died.

Children of the Robert Scott family were: Thomas (1830-1877) who married Clara Willard of Ironton, Ohio, Alice, who married Harry Spear, Fannie, who married Harry Gardner, Nannie (1845-1896), who married Marshall Field, George, who married Addie Ellison of Ironton, Nora, Rozzie and Jennie (unmarried), and Harry G., who married Sarah Clark. Of these, Alice, her husband and a daughter Catherine were residents of Greenup for a few years and attended the Greenup Academy as did also Harry G. Scott in the late 1870's. Nannie and Marshall Field I, who established the large mercantile house in Chicago, were married at Mount Vernon Furnace. When he came to visit the Scott home before the marriage, a tragedy occurred when Jennie was burned fatally by the explosion of a lamp in the home.

Marshall and Nannie Scott Field were the parents of Marshall II, who married Albertine Huck of Chicago and succeeded his father in the mercantile business, and of Ethel who married (1) Arthur Tree of England and (2) Admiral David Beatty when Lord Beatty was a captain in the British Navy. Nannie Field died at Nice, France, where she had gone for her health, February 27, 1896.

In the year 1956 another chapter was added to the Robert Scott family records. Marshall Field III, born in Chicago September 28, 1893, died November 8th in New York.[1] Mr. Field married (1) Evelyn Marshall in 1916. They were the parents of three children, Marshall IV, Barbara and Bettina. He married (2) Ruth Phipps and their children are Phyllis and Fiona. Mr. Field was actively connected with the *Sun* and *Times* Company of Chicago, as well as the Marshall Field Mercantile Company.

The people of this section have always been interested in the

[1] NOTE: The author had some interesting correspondence with Marshall Field III when getting material for *A History of Greenup County.*

doings of the Scott family. A sister of Nannie Scott Field, Nora, made her home with the family for many years and was well remembered in the will of Marshall I.

Trimble

David Trimble was born in 1782. He was a son of John and Amy Trimble, of Frederick County, Virginia. Other members of the family were John, William, Isaac, Ann Woodrow and Sarah Starr. David was a graduate of William and Mary College, in 1799. He served in the War of 1812. He studied law and practiced at Mount Sterling, Kentucky. He came to Greenup County where he was elected to the state legislature, serving from 1836-1839.

In 1818, David and John Trimble, with Richard Deering, built a furnace at Argillite, the first in the county. In 1833, he and others built Raccoon Furnace. In the latter 1820's he bought the square containing Lots No. 1, 2, 3 and 4 and razed the log homes of James McGuire, Thomas Richards and the Halley family. He built the large frame house on Lot No. 1 that was the Trimble-Stark property for more than seventy years. At the death of the latter owner the square was sold and the new owners sold that part of it where the jail stands to the county and other parts to those who have built on it. The horse block that stood at the front gate of the large house has been moved nearer to the corner. Of these there were three others in the town, at the Kouns Tavrn, at the Dr. Alfred Spalding home and at the Robert Callihan tavern on Main Street. The Spalding family had theirs moved to their new home.

David Trimble died at Greenup in 1842 and is buried in the Greenup Cemetery at the right and near the top of the driveway. A few years ago the Colonial Dames of Kentucky replaced his gravestone with a larger one. Near his grave is that of Charles Wilson, who was connected with the Trimble furnace at Raccoon. Mr. Trimble made a will in 1832 and added a codicil in 1836, which in part reads, "To my nephew John T. Woodrow, I leave one fourth of my new furnace on Raccoon and one fourth of 20,000 acres of land, including the furnace." Mr. Trimble was a charter member of the Greenup Masonic Lodge.

Walker

The Samuel Walker family of Virginia came down the Ohio River on a flatboat in 1812. They stopped at what has since been known as Walker Landing, near what is Siloam now. Among their children were Hannah, who was born in 1800 in Virginia and married Nathaniel Warner in 1825 (see Warner family), James, who married Nancy, one of the seven daughters of Aaron Kinney of Portsmouth, Ohio and who lived on the farm. They built a very modern brick home for that period where they reared four children, William, Samuel, Mary and Peter Kinney. William married Ella, daughter of John T. and Lydia Tanner King. Both William and his wife died leaving two young children, Roy and May, both of whom went to California. Samuel married Lizzie Bahner and Mary married William Burns and moved to Califorina. Roy and May, mentioned above, lived with them for some time. Peter Kinney married Mary Warner and after his death she and her family moved to Louisville. Samuel, a third son, married Anna Lawson.

Warner (Taylor J. Warner)

The Warner family emigrated from England to Boston, Massachusetts, in the late 1700's. Nathaniel Warner came to Pennsylvania and from there down the Ohio River by flatboat to Kentucky. He stopped at Walker Landing. The Walker family had come from Virginia in 1812. A daughter Hannah, born in Virginia August 1, 1800, and Nathaniel Warner were married December 26, 1825. Nathaniel died in 1850, age sixty years, and Hannah died March 11, 1879. They always lived near Walker Landing and are buried in the Mount Zion Churchyard. Mr. Warner was one of the original trustees of the Mount Zion Church.

Nathaniel II, son of Nathaniel and Hannah Walker, married Jerusha, a daughter of Charles and Jane Berry Middaugh, of Tygart. Their children were Nathaniel, George, Fannie Casteel, Sallie Mullins, Nannie Lavender, Mary Walker and Taylor Jackson. Of these children, Nathaniel III married Leah Mullins, George married Minnie Burkhardt, Charles married Minnie Palmer and Taylor married Winnie Lamblin. Most of these families have moved to other places. Children of Taylor and Winnie Lamblin Warner are Norman, Charlotte and Roscoe. Norman and Roscoe served in World War II. Roscoe was killed in an auto accident in 1948. Other children of Nathaniel and Hannah Walker were George, who married Levina M. Gammon and moved to Kansas in the late 1870's or early 1880's, Sarah Ann who married William Jones, Fannie who married Stephen Lawson, and Elizabeth who married John Wilson Gammon. Hannah, a daughter of George and Lovina Gammon Warner, returned to Greenup County and married Morton McCoy. They went to West Virginia to make their home. A second daughter, Mary Ellen, married John Van Bibber, son of John and Lydia Tanner King, who went to Kansas and returned with his bride. These two couples had been childhood sweethearts before the Warner family moved to Kansas. Van, as he was known, died in a few years and his wife returned to the home in Kansas. Other children of this family were Samuel, Taylor and Betty.

XII

Villages and Towns

Early VILLAGES of the county were Argillite, Beattyville, Coal Branch, Danleyton, Mount Zion (Frost), Fullerton, Gray's Branch, Hopewill, Hunnewell, Limeville Lynn Oldtown Palmyra, Raceland, Russell, Short Branch, Siloam, Smith Branch, Springville (South Portsmouth), and Wurtland. The greater number of these have, as they had in early days, names of early settlers living in or near them. The greatest changes have been made in those along the river. Russell became an important place with the construction of the Chesapeake and Ohio Railroad and has overflowed into the villages of Flatwoods, Worthington and Raceland. The last-named was platted by Benjamin Chinn in the early 1900's and was known as Chinnville until a race track was constructed in 1920's and the name changed to Raceland.

Mount Zion became Frost with a post office and railroad station, the name being changed because of confusion of a station, Mount Zion, on the Louisville & Nashville Railroad. Springville became South Portsmouth by the new railroad. Fullerton grew from a small village to a place of importance after the construction of the road. South Shore is expanding into an important town extending from Tygart Creek west to Fullerton. Below Springville (South Portsmouth) a town was platted by Reuben Thomson, in 1849, was known as Beattyville for a few years, and is now a part of South Portsmouth.

Raceland

Raceland and its surrounding towns and outlying communities are built on part of a five-thousand-acre "Grant of Land" to Abraham Buford from Virginia after the Revolutionary War. After a lawsuit with a man named Blaine over the land, which was won by Buford, he gave it to his son Charles, who some time later sold it in farming tracts.

Raceland is about a mile west of Russell and about the same from the Ohio River. The Chesapeake and Ohio Railroad is located between the river and the town. It has, according to the 1960 census, a population of 1,115. It has paved streets, water, telephone, gas and power facilities, also a modern sewage disposal system. The community operates three schools with the high school in the town. There are five churches and many nice homes.

About the year 1790, Joseph and Nancy Powell, with several children, came from Virginia and settled on Buford land. In 1812, two other families from Virginia settled near the Powell family. One of these was Benjamin and Elizabeth Brown Mead with their ten children. Elizabeth Mead still owns and lives on a portion of the pioneer land. The third pioneer family was that of John and Sophia Brown Chinn, with four children. The Chinn family acquired a great deal of the Buford land and, consisting of merchants as well as farmers, laid off a portion of the land in lots which became known as Chinnville. In the 1920's, J. C. Keene and a party of men from Lexington constructed a race track and the name was changed to Raceland. After a few years, the race track was abandoned and the land is now used for farming. New homes are being built on the race-track land.

Flatwoods

The town of Flatwoods is built on high-level land at the rear of Russell. It was a thinly settled community until the construction of the Chesapeake and Ohio Railroad, when the population of Russell overflowed into other communities. As it stands today, Flatwoods has far outgrown the mother town. Its population, according to the 1960 census, numbers 3,741, while that of Russell totals 1,458. It has nice churches and homes with all of the facilities of a modern town.

Three furnaces were in operation in early days, Bellefonte (1826), Amanda (1829) and Caroline (1833). These gave employment to many of the people of the area. Pioneer families were those of Abraham Hamor, Samuel Patterson and Henry Williams (from Pennsylvania). Abraham Hamor was manager of Bellefont Furnace. The community of Bellefonte is built on the site of the old furnace and has a population of 337. A country club with a golf course has been in existence for many years.

In recent years a hospital has been built near Bellefonte.

Lloyd

The old settlement of Smith Branch is fast growing into the town of Lloyd. It is located on both sides of the Branch—the eastern part on the former Dr. Rom Biggs farm, the western on the Thomas Biggs land—both of which have been laid off into lots in recent years. It extends almost to Gray's Branch where the Greenup Dam, which gives employment to residents, is located. Two large stores have been built, one on either side of the Branch. A Baptist church has been built and ground purchased for a Methodist church on the western section. Farming remains the principal occupation of the people.

A modern home for indigents of the county was built on the eastern side of the Branch, in 1959. The larger county home and farm, constructed over one hundred years ago and no longer suitable, were sold by the county and the smaller, modern home built.

South Shore

South Shore is built on a land grant to Josiah Morton, a Revolutionary War soldier. Descendants still reside on a portion of this grant, which extended from Tygart Creek to Stoner Hill on the west. Before the 1880's there were but four houses on the western section of the grant, the eastern section being in farming lands in use. With the construction of the Chesapeake and Ohio Railroad in the late 1880's, the western portion began to grow in population. Farmers came from Tygart Valley, among them the Warnock, Fullerton and other Morton families, members of which became merchants. At the close of the century the town of Fullerton was established.

The location of Fullerton is on a narrow area lying between the Ohio River and the hills, it extended its growth to the east and west. On the east it has grown into the town of South Shore. The largest industry is the Taylor Brickyard, which employs local labor. Others are employed across the Ohio River at the Norfolk and Western shops and at the steel mills.

South Shore has many nice homes, paved streets and all facilities for pleasant living. Handsome brick churches have succeeded the Methodist and Baptist frame buildings of Fullerton. A post office was built in recent years. Also, a Masonic Hall, the first floor of which houses the Bank; an American Legion building with its ball park; a drug store, and a large department store, and a new Fire Department building are under construction. The WIOI broadcasting station is located on the Forrest King farm above the town.

East of Greenup

Through the decades 1870-1880-1890, East Greenup was known as "Over the Rhine." The town of Greenup was dry territory and beer was sold by a German family just over the "Rhine Bridge" where imbibing citizens could procure drink. Later this property was bought by Adam Frey who built the present residence and a store building for hardware. Two frame cottages stood between this and the frame house on the corner above, which was built and occupied by the B. F. Lacock family during the decades. Across the alley is a large frame house, built by Ab Taylor, a lumberman, who in the early 1880's moved to Tennessee. This property changed owners many times until bought by B. F. Kidwell for a home. The W. M. Stevens frame home has been converted into an apartment house.

Above the next alley are three brick houses, two of which were built in the 1870's by George Ward and Thomas Sweeny, brick masons. These were occupied by the builders, George Ward who married India, a daughter of Mr. and Mrs. George Pratt, and Thomas Sweeney who married Nellie Vincent, of the Myers family. The third house was built by William Hord, of Ashland, and the family lived there a number of years. Above these stood the Mrs. Kate Eifort home, which was the last house on the south side of East Greenup.

On the north side of Main Street in East Greenup near the Rhine Bridge is a cottage built by George Corum where he and his father, William Corum, lived a few years in the 1880's and which became the home of the Ab McCoy family for a number of years. The next cottage was built by Mr. and Mrs. Albert Shilling, and above it was a cottage built by the H. B. Woodrow family, who edited the *Greenup Gazette* in the late 1870's. A double house owned by R. B. Nickell stood on the corner, and across the alley was a frame house built by James Warnock in the 1870's. Many nice homes have been built above these since the 1890's. Among these are the McCoy, Corum, Kilgore, Elam, Taft and others, until it is difficult to tell where East Greenup ends and Riverton begins. Above the site of the old Eastern Kentucky Railroad are many homes built on original Hockaday land. The Greenup High School is located here.

At the rear of East Greenup are the homes of many Negro families. The McConnell, King and Martin families came from the farms above Greenup, after the Civil War. The church and school are located here.

Riverton is built on the original farms of Jesse Boone, Andrew Hood and John Hockaday. Riverton came into existence with the Eastern Kentucky Railroad through eastern capitalists, who also built an office, hotel and a home for the manager, H. W. Bates. In the late 1870's, George Hockaday built the large frame house above Town Branch which has been the William McKee family home for years. Other homes have been built on Front Street between the McKee and Bates homes, and in recent years a frame house has been built by J. L. O'Brien at the head of this street.

From Main Street in Greenup many nice homes line the way to White Oak Crossing, the last one on the north side being that of Hon. J. B. Bates. These homes, from Town Branch to White Oak Crossing, stand on the original Boone, Howe, and later, Hockaday farms. Above here are early farms of the Martin, Smith, Collins, Jacobs, Cochran and Brammer families, and much of the land remains in use for farm purposes. A large part of the John McConnell land is occupied by the Dupont and King Powder Plants.

Beyond these is the town of Wurtland which was in early days the home of the Fulton Forge and Oil Works. The first merchant in Greenup County was Benjamin Chinn, who operated a store near which stands the store of Wurts Chinn, a descendant. Above Wurtland are original farms of Chinn, Mead and Powell, on parts of which Raceland stands. Near are the villages of Worthington and Melrose, which are overflows from the town of Russell, which became a very important town with the coming of the Chesapeake and Ohio Railroad in the late 1880's. Below Russell a road leads to Flatwoods, another overflow from the town. Above Russell many new homes form Riverview. Above here between Russell and Ashland were two furnaces. Bellefont, built in 1826, and Amanda, in 1820, both by Poage men. The Poage family were large land owners and were interested in affairs of Greenup County before Boyd County was formed in 1860. A road leads to Bellefont from the highway below Ashland. Bellefont is growing into quite a large place with many beautiful homes.

The Jean Seaton, William and Jesse Corum homes in the rear of Riverton were built many years before the three decades. The Jesse Corum home burned in the 1870's and the Seaton home in the 1890's. The William Corum brick house is owned and occupied by the Sam Leslie family. A small home stands near the old Seaton house. A brick house was built by the B. F. Bennett family on the site of the Jesse Corum home in the late 1870's. Many new homes have been built on this rise during the years, some of them by the Collins, Crawford, Taylor and Fullerton families. A frame building, built by the Hockaday family, stands now at the curve of the bypass which joins the highway near.

From the rear of Riverton, a road passes the W. Hollow, Jesse Stuart, Collins and Reeves farms to Argillite where, in 1848, was located Pennsylvania Furnace and later the Hoop lumber and flour mill, and a tie yard. This road leads to Oldtown, once a very important place, being the center of Laurel, Buffalo and Hopewell Furnaces. A store operated by Stark, Kouns and Womack in the 1840's is still a going concern operated by the Orin Womack family. On the right, from Argillite to Oldtown, are the homes of the Virgin and Downs families, whose descendants live on land settled by these families about 1807. In 1800, John Downs and Lucy Virgin were married at Cincinnati and settled near the Rezin Virgin family on the north fork of Oldtown Creek.

South of Greenup

From Washington Street beyond Perry, across the Chesapeake and Ohio Railroad and the bypass, were Seaton-Spalding and later Warnock farms. This road once led to the Falls of Little Sandy, a favorite camping and fishing place, which has been greatly changed by nature through the years. Near here were the farms of the Archer Womack, Kaut and Diedrich families. Across the Little Sandy River Bridge stood Raccoon Furnace, built and operated by David and John Trimble. When the furnace was no longer in existence the land was bought by Col. William Worthington, who lived there until 1880. Lying between Raccoon and Argillite is the Clay Lick community of farmers. In this area Greenbo Lake is being built. Before the Chesapeake and Ohio Railroad was built, the Dr. William S. Kouns home was the only one between the Raccoon road and Laurel Alley. Since then homes have been built by Matt Warnock, Scott Warnock and Elwood Kinner, and occupied by members of the families. Other homes have been built above and below these mentioned.

Several roads lead from Greenup up Tygart Creek, one of these beginning at Frost, passing the William Biggs land, the old Mount Zion Church, the farms of the Lawson, Hitchcock, Ware, Glover and Foster families, on which descendants of the Lawson, Hitchcock and Glover families are still living. Beyond this community is one settled by the Coleman, Craycraft, McClave and Greenslate families, which was known as Culpepper in early days. Dr. James M. Moore, a native of Ireland, came to this community in the 1860's. He married Elizabeth Craycraft and practiced his profession in Tygart until the late 1870's, when he moved to Ironton where he was a practicing physician until his death.

Beyond the last area mentioned above were two furnaces, Enterprise, built in 1832, and Globe, in 1833. A covered wooden bridge, known as Enterprise Bridge, crossed Tygart Creek and was dismantled a few years ago. Near the east entrance of the bridge stood the Raike watermill, probably the last of its kind in the county. A community known as Plum Fork was the home of Warnock, Stewart and Nickells families. Beyond this settlement were the homes of the Bennett families. Bennetts Mill was operated in the 1860's by these families. The long, covered wooden bridge, still in use here, was built in 1850.

Between Bennetts Mill and Lynn are farms once owned by Moseley, Jones and Bagby families, which have had many different owners since. Lynn was an important early village, being the site of a shoe factory and of tanneries. A post office, Lynn, was established here at a very early time. In 1850, the Liberty Christian Church was built on land donated by Rival Jones to the following members, Pratt, Brooks, Moseley, Pugh and Jones, "for as long as the sweet water flows and the green grass grows." The foundation stones may be seen on the Moseley-Dupuy farm. O. N. Jones was a long-time pastor of this church. Dr. Charles Secrest lived near the church and practiced his profession over a large area during the decades.

Beyond this settlement were farms of several Waring families, where in 1790 Thomas Waring came from Mason County and bought one thousand acres of land. The Liberty Methodist Church is built on land donated by John and Ursula Waring to five trustees, Charles Craycraft, Edward Stephenson, Basil Waring, Moses F. Dupuy and I. S. Canterbury. Of these only Dupuy families live and farm here. The Howlands also are descendants of Charles Howland, who bought a large tract of land from the State of Virginia, brought many slaves and settled on Tygart Creek where Howland families still live. Quite a bit farther up Tygart and its branches were the Morton, Warnock, Van Bibber, Meadows, Holbrooks, McGinness, Baker, Smith and Logan farms, with descendants still owning some of the original land.

In 1820, General Robert Pogue bought 80,000 acres of land in the county which, at that time, included a part of what is now Carter County. Descendants living on the original land are the Cooper and Duncan families in Greenup County. This section is the headquarters of the Texas-Tennessee Gas Company. Post offices in this section are Warnock, Load and Kehoe. Toward the southwestern part of the county are Buffalo, Grassy and Three Prong Creeks. There were two furnaces here, New Hampshire, built by Sam Seaton in 1838, and Kenton, by John Waring in 1856.

West of Greenup

At the February term of the newly organized county court, in 1804, a motion was made by Jesse Boone that John Mackoy, Andrew Hood, Josiah Davidson and Andrew Wolf be appointed to view the necessary and best way to open a road from the county line opposite the mouth of the Scioto (then two miles below the present mouth) to the Big Sandy River. The road west began at the Little Sandy River and ran to the brick house on the Rankins farm, where it turned north to the Ohio River. This was changed when the Chesapeake and Ohio Railroad was built. For years there were but three houses between Little Sandy and the Rankins home. These were the William Warnock, a one-and-one-half-story brick home, the James Bryan, a two-story brick, and the frame cottage of the James Hockaday family. From the old Rankins home a road built in later years leads to Short Branch and Whetstone.

Upon the rise, at the left of the highway, stood the frame home of the Hinton-Hawkins families which was destroyed and a new one built on the site. At Coal Branch the road turned to the left for a short distance, crossed a south-to-north covered bridge to the main highway. This road connected with the Tygart Creek Highway, passing the homes of the Richards, Burton, Wills, Pugh and Lennington families. Between Coal and Smith Branches stood the Coaling store, near where charcoal was burned and shipped on barges to Kelly Mills at Ironton, Ohio. The farming section began below here, the first farm being that of Dr. R. C. Biggs. Below Smith Branch was the farm and homestead of William Biggs, Sr., which later became the property of the Thomas Biggs, Sr., family. The John Taylor Lawson farm adjoined the Biggs farm on the west. This became the property of Taylor Lawson who sold it to F. M. Warnock who, in turn, sold it to the government for the dam located there. The town of Lloyd is being built on these two farms.

Farms lying between the above-mentioned farms and Gray's Branch were owned and operated by the Reid, Bryan, Culver and Bryson families into the 1870's and 1880's, and have changed owners several times since then. The fine old brick home of the James Bryson family was razed a few years ago and a modern home built on the site. The Presbyterian Church was organized and a church built in 1829. This church was razed in 1881 and a new one built. In 1919, the church was sold to a Christian Church congregation. Below here were Waring, Hill, Morton, Riggs and Jones farms. The roller dam is under construction at this place.

The road leading from here to Rocky has been changed, with a fill taking the place of the old covered bridge. Near here were the long-time farms of the McNeal and Gray families. Limeville, below Rocky, was once a very busy place, making and shipping lime by boat up and down the river. Old-time residents were the Dr. Munn family, the Duval, Tong, Merrill, West, Cartwright and Young families. Descendants of the Tong and West families have homes on the original land. Below Limeville the Obadiah Mackoy land extended almost to Siloam. That part near Limeville was bought by the Merrill and Young families and is, at present, the property of the Volney Thomson family.

Adjoining the Obadiah Mackoy land were the farms of the pioneer John Mackoy, whose descendants lived at Siloam until later years. John Mackoy sold his farm to the King Dameron family, Lavinia Dugan Ware sold her land to the Matt Gammon family in the decades. Until late years the Henry Mackoy farm was owned by members of the family. The Henry Mackoy homestead stands near the river and is in excellent condition. This part is owned now by the May family, while the lower sections have become the property of the McKell, Seelhorst and Hardin families.

The large frame house up on the Siloam hill, once the home of the John Johnston family, is now owned and occupied by members of the Hardin family. Other sections of the Johnston farms are owned by the McKell and Seelhorst families, who have built modern homes on the land. The Christian Church, built on Mackoy land in the 1840's, burned in the early 1900's, and the present one stands on the site. Another, to house a Union church, has been built in recent years. The Samuel Walker farm adjoined the

Mackoy land on the west. Samuel's son, James, built the two-story brick house. This farm was bought by the William Harper family, of Portsmouth, Ohio, who resided there a number of years. On other Mackoy land are the present farms of the Bush, Newberry, Martin and Hardin families. The Green Richards family operated a general store here in the early 1900's.

The community of Frost was known as Mount Zion until the name was changed by the Chesapeake and Ohio Railroad and goverment in early 1900. This community, through the three decades, consisted of the Robert Johnson, George Warner, William Gammon and Volney Thomson homes, on what is known now as Sand Hill. At the foot of Sand Hill the road has been changed from the original, farther to the north. The William Biggs, Benjamin F. King and other King farms lay between Sand Hill and Tygart Creek. The Benjamin F. King farm was bought by the Judd family of Ashland in the early 1950's. In 1956, the Chesapeake and Ohio Railroad Realty Company began buying land here and the Biggs, Judd, Lawson and Robinson land lying between the C. & O. R.R. and the Ohio River was bought by that company.

The Taylor King farm west of the above farms is occupied by the community of Upper King's Addition. The original James King farm is the property of the Carl Morton family. The John King farm at the mouth of Tygart is the original Thomas B. King, pioneer home. The log home was razed about 1878 and the present brick one built by John King, whose son, Forrest, owns and occupies it. Lower King's Addition, McKell High and Grade School are built on original Thomas B. King land, which became the property of the son Benjamin, father of the above-mentioned.

The Josiah Morton land, a Virginia Revolutionary War grant, began at the west bank of Tygart Creek and extended to below the present town of Fullerton. Morton descendants own and live on parts of this land. The Taylor Brickyard and South Shore are built on the grant. In the decades of 1870-1880-1890 there were few dwellings within the present limits of the town, the oldest ones being that of Harrison Fullerton, situated on the river bank, and the two-story frame house in the center of the town. This was the property of the Music family until bought by the Frank Bennett family about 1898. The George Winn family occupied this home when Mr. Winn brought the *Thomas O'Neil* from Greenup to enter the ferry trade between Fullerton and Portsmouth in 1898.

With the coming of the Chesapeake and Ohio Railroad many

families moved here from Tygart Valley. Among them were Fullertons (Harvey), Warnocks, Taylors, Meadowses, Holbrooks, and Bennetts. In 1895 Clyde King established a brick yard. At the end of the decades, many homes had been built and a post office established, stores of Warnock and Morton families were in operation and a school had been built.

South Portsmouth (Springville) was the first settlement in the county. The pioneers were the Thomson, Lawson, Arnold, Zuhars, Brooker, McCallister, and Anderson families with descendants still living here. With the building of the C. & O. R.R., the old homes near the river bank were razed. The new village of Beattyville came into existence in 1849 and a Methodist church, the present one, was built (1876) to succeed the small building nearby. Below here, on the Patrick Henry Revolutionary War grant, were the farms of the Kellen, Thomson, Bagby, McElheny and Laughlin families. Descendants of several of these families live on the original lands of those named above. Thomson farms adjoined in Greenup and Lewis Counties, with an old barn still standing on the line. This is the end of the Greenup County road, established by the court February, 1804, which has been changed very little since that time.

XIII

Greenupsburg and Greenup—1870-1880-1890

FROM ITS organization in 1804 to 1872 the county seat was Greenupsburg. In 1872, the *burg* was omitted officially, but for many years it was known locally by the original name.

In 1872 James Gilruth, a native of the French Grant, across the Ohio River, whose family had migrated to Iowa in early days, wrote in a letter to his friend, Gen. W. H. Kelly, about the settlement on both sides of the river. Of the Kentucky side he wrote, among other things, "The first house on the site of Greenupsburg was built by Lewis Wilcoxen above the mouth of the Little Sandy River." He wrote of the Hood, Howe, Boone, and Nichols families that had settled along the river above the Wilcoxen home, a great deal of which is contained in *A History of Greenup County*.

In 1895, Mr. Johnny Myers wrote an article concerning early settlers, homes and buildings of the town as he had known them. Much of his material is contained in the above-mentioned history.

In 1956, Nina Mitchell Biggs wrote of the town as she knew it during the decades of 1870-1880-1890. She was born at the close of the Civil War, when it was the principal topic of conversation and a great deal of controversy, with citizens siding with their own section, north or south, and there was tension in the air with bitter feelings engendered between neighbors and friends. Time has healed many of these since men of north and south have fought in the world wars of this century.

The River

As the Ohio River was the most important factor in the settlement of Greenup County, so it continued to be in its development. Settlers and needed supplies were constantly coming down the river, and after a few years farmers transported surpluses to other places. Monied men from eastern states became interested in the Ohio as a transportation route to New Orleans. In 1810, the Ohio Steamboat Company was formed at Pittsburgh and in 1811 the first boat, *New Orleans*, was launched there. On reaching Louisville she was tied up the day of the earthquake, December 6, 1811. Others were soon built and in a few years both passenger and towboats were traveling the river.

Men interested in iron-making came down the river from Pennsylvania and began building furnaces as early as 1818 where necessary materials were found. Iron-making increased river traffic, both passenger and freight, which reached the peak during the 1870's and 1880's, when the beautiful side-wheelers, *Bostona, Fleetwood, Telegraph, Potomac, Bonanza*, and the less beautiful stern-wheelers, *Granite State, Keystone State, Andes, Emma Graham* and the several *Ohios*, of which *Ohio No. 4* was a side-wheeler, plied the river between Pittsburgh and Cincinnati. Daily packets, the *Fannie Dugan, City of Ironton, Minnie Bay, Lizzie Johnson, Scioto* and the little one-deck *Fashion*, all built by local river men, carried mail, passengers and light freight between Portsmouth and Pomeroy. Towboats came into use, the *Condor* being the first one built, carrying coal from the mountains. A few people who remember these view with pleasure the *Omar*, one of the very few "old-timers" of the three decades 1870, 1880, 1890. Also, some few may remember the *Storm*, a boat true to her name, which was placed on the river to carry mail in the flood of 1883. It caused so much damage to property along the banks by the huge waves it created that it was soon stopped.

Of all the boats that plied the river during these decades the most popular were the seven *Telegraphs*, the last one being built in 1890 at Harmon, Ohio, by the White Collar Line Company. The Chesapeake and Ohio Railroad was finished in the early 1890's, and took a great deal of trade from the river. About the middle of the 1890's the *Telegraph No. 7* was placed in the Cincinnati-Louisville trade and was wrecked on a dark stormy night, November 27, 1897, at Twelve Pole Island, near Louisville. Her musical whistle, which had been heard up and down the river for so many years from the several boats of the name, is said to be lying at the bottom of the river near Twelve Pole Island. The following lines taken from a poem written by Garnet Laidlaw Eskew in 1929 bring memories of those splendid river boats of the three decades:

They wore a strange beauty all their own—
Those mighty river boats that I have known
And have long lost—save that I still find
Their mirrored images within my mind.

Other craft that plied the river were the showboats, trading boats and shantyboats, making the river front a very interesting place to the little river town. The showboats, "floating palaces," were towed by a small steamboat and stopped at all small towns. The first I have known of these was *French's Sensation,* in 1883. The narrow river grade was occupied by the wharfboat and the ferry landing. Mr. French had known my grandmother before the Civil War and came to see her. The boat landed in front of her home. Mr. French gave tickets to the family. My father took all of the children old enough to attend a show. I was teaching in the country and so missed the show but heard plenty about it when I came home. *French's New Sensation, Sunny South* and *Golden Rod* were others I have known of since that first one. Trading boats carrying table- and glassware landed exchanging their wares for rags and iron. Shantyboats carrying families tied up along the bank, sometimes for a whole summer. The ferry *Royal* was operated between Greenup and Haverhill during the earliest of the decades, the *O'Neil* in the 1890's. The latter was taken to the Fullerton-Portsmouth trade by Captain George Winn in 1893. Skiffs and johnboats owned by Greenup and Haverhill people were tied along the banks.

Shipping on the river in early days was a hazardous business, depending mostly on the stage of the river, which in dry seasons became so low that at our town it could be forded on horseback, and again so high, as in the floods of 1883-1884 and again in 1913 and 1937, that it caused a great loss to those engaged in the trade. In 1920 Congress appropriated the money to provide a nine-foot stage, by building dams, forty-eight in number, from Pittsburgh to Cairo, a distance of over 950 miles. These small dams have been outgrown by the immense traffic and are being succeeded by roller dams. These may, by being spaced with great distance between, cause not only shipping to increase but also river travel, if only for pleasure, to stage a comeback.

For more than fifty years pig iron was shipped from the many furnaces throughout the county by boat to Pittsburgh. When furnace days were over much pig iron was stacked on the river grade and on vacant lots on Perry Street where it remained until in the 1880's. By this time the raising and shipping of livestock and other farm products to Cincinnati markets had increased greatly. Livestock was herded on the river grade. The boat crew would unroll a sort of fence made of staves and heavy material, surround the stock and drive it across the wharf to the boat. This was very interesting to the townfolk, especially when there was stock of all kinds to be shipped.

The Town

In 1870 the population of Greenupsburg was 507. There were but six streets, all other thoroughfares being known as alleys. There were three churches, Methodist, Christian and Presbyterian. Sunday school was held in the morning at the first two and in the afternoon at the last, which was a good arrangement for all concerned. Church services were held in all of them morning and evening, with prayer meetings on different evenings during the week. Union Christmas celebrations and temperance meetings were held in the courthouse. Methodist women had missionary meetings, socials and sewing circles. On Saturday night A Mite Society was held at the home of a member where young people could meet and play games from seven o'clock until nine o'clock. Church members as a rule did not sanction dancing. However, there were balls given by the Masons, which were well attended by many of the townfolk and by the families of the furnace owners and managers. These were held in the long dining hall of the Kouns House until the completion of the Masonic Temple about 1867. Many of the young people of the town continued to use the Kouns House hall until 1883, when Joseph Pfaff built the one on Harrison Street, long known as Pfaff's Hall, for the pleasure of the young people.

Besides the events mentioned above, the courthouse was the scene of school exhibitions, debates, and a great religious revival when George O. Barnes came to the town in 1880, and also a temperance meeting, in 1878, when everyone in the town—except those who should have—signed the "pledge." Many people from other nearby towns attended the Barnes Revival. He carried a portable organ which was played by his daughter Marie. Many new songs came into use, as did Mr. Barnes's favorite expression, "Praise the Lord," which he used often and fervently.

The new school auditorium was completed in 1881 and the school plays were staged there. Traveling troupes also gave such performances as "Ten Nights In A Bar Room," "East Lynn," and such other sorts of exhibitions as sleight-of-hand and juggling.

When I first remember the town there were brick pavements, but the streets between were dusty in summer and muddy in winter. Few families owned horses and buggies. Even doctors with country patients rode horseback. Depending on the condition of the roads, country folks came to town by horseback, express or by wagon, the horses being hitched to racks built for the purpose around the courthouse square. Many years have passed between that time and the present, when the square is surrounded by parking meters.

Residents of the town reached manhood and womanhood knowing the streets as Front, Elizabeth, Main and "Back" Street instead of Perry. In 1954, the council erected markers with the names of streets as they appeared on the first known "plat" of the town. Two exceptions are Boston Alley, now Ash Street, and Jefferson, which was added later. East Greenup was known as "Over The Rhine" when I first knew it, and Ricerton was a small town in itself.

David Trimble, an early furnace man, in 1818 bought the four lots on Water (Front) Street between Washington and Cedar Alley. He razed the log houses and built a three-story house at the Corner of Washington and Front, which was known during the three decades as the Stark property. Below Cedar Alley stood the John Passmore Tanner home and a cabinet shop. These burned about 1869 or 1870 and were not rebuilt. Below this were two cottages, the homes of James Rankins and John Ferguson. A large log house owned by the Basenback family stood next to these, and the lot is now occupied by the home of Renard Staph. Below Walnut Alley, on the river bank, was the very old home of Jacob Cochran. On the lower side of Walnut Alley stood the "Fifteenth Amendment," a long, narrow, red frame building that was built after the Civil War for Negro families.

The old foundry on the corner of Elizabeth Street and Cherry Alley now houses the Kinner Lumber Company. Below this and the old Ferry Lot still stands the George Mefford frame cottage, looking much as it did in the decades. On the old Ferry Lot stood a cooper shop, owned by Pratt and Brooks, in the 1870's and early 1880's. The cottage on the corner of the cooper yard was occupied by the foreman, Mr. Kirkpatrick. Above Cherry Alley on Main were the cottages of the Warnock and Ferguson family and from Walnut to Cedar Alley there stood four one-story houses, owned and occupied by Benjamin Smith, John Powell, B. F. Brown and Robert Robb. Above Cedar Alley stands a brick house, red originally, built by Dr. Samuel Ellis in the late 1840's or early 1850's. In the 1870's Dr. Ellis sold it to the John Schmutz family, and it is now the property of the County Educational Board.

Dr. Ellis built and occupied for many years the present Kinner home. Above this is an old-time cottage built in 1839, as Mr. Myers wrote. During the decades it housed the families of Jeremiah Davidson, Dr. A. G. Sellards, Sydney Van Bibber, James Womack (who was school superintendent in 1875, later moving to Texas), and, in the early 1880's, the Dr. M. S. Leslie family. On the south side of Main Street, near Little Sandy, stood two cottages, homes of Mrs. Lydia Warnock and the John Riggs family. The two-story frame across Cherry Alley was built by James Rankins in the late 1870's, and was later the Clarence Lacock home. Above a modern cottage built by Ralph Leslie stands a two-story frame house built in the 1870's by Bernard Kuehborth, a lumberman. He sold it to J. W. Kouns, who later sold it to John T. Womack, and it is now the property of Mr. and Mrs. Buford Myers. On the corner, across Walnut Alley, is a brick home built by Thomas H. Paynter, lawyer and congressman, in 1878. This became the property of the Robert Wilson family, and in late years has become property of the Presbyterian Church which occupies the lot above it.

A two-story frame house above the church stands on the site of one built in very early days by Frank York, and has been occupied by Jacob Thornsburry, F. B. Trussell, and J. T. Lawson. It was also for many years the Dr. M. S. Leslie family home. The frame house on the corner of Cedar Alley was built in furnace days, and in the 1879's was occupied by the Mrs. Addie Jones family, later by the Scott Warnock family, and then it became the property of the Dock Fullerton family. Across Cedar Alley was the Andes Tavern, kept by the Robert Callihan family, the upper part being occupied by the Van Puthoph family. This became the property of the Willis family, and, when the tavern was destroyed by fire, a member of the family built a home on the lot.

Above the Andes Tavern stood a one-story brick, the home of Professor J. B. Norris, where he taught a private school during the 1870's and early 1880's. On this site Dr. R. C. Biggs built the frame house which is now the Riggs Funeral Home. The lot above, which was vacant for years, is occupied by the Shepherd-West Hardware Store. This building was built by C. B. Bennett to house Ford Motors. On the corner of Main and Washington Streets there stood in the early 1870's, and for many years, a small frame building, home of the halter shop of Hobbs and Lewis. This was bought by James M. Sowards, who in the middle 1870's built a brick store building on the site and his frame residence below it. The building burned and was rebuilt by J. Watt and John T. Womack as it stands today. They operated a general store from this site for more than sixty years. It is now owned and occupied by the Moccabee Dry Goods Store.

On Perry Street between Little Sandy and Cherry Alley are two cottages that before the three decades were owned and occupied by the John Schmutz and Thomas Brooks families. Above these, in excellent condition, is the old Joseph Pollock home, built probably in the middle 1850's. Between this home and Washington Street were the homes of the Negro families, Chillison, Thomas, Beach, Waring and Warnock. On Washington beyond Perry were the homes of the Green and Wheatley families, also the Negro church and school. Perry Street was known in early days as Back Street. Continuing up Perry Street, the James McMullen home stood on the east corner of Washington, and on the corner of Harrison is the large frame house built by Basil Warnock in the later 1870's, which has always been owned and occupied by members of the Warnock family.

Across Perry Street is a frame house built by the Robert Wilson, Sr., family, which was later the Travis Kendall home. On an early "platt" of Greenupsburg there are two lots marked "Warnick." In 1815, the Greenup Academy was built on these lots. It was a long narrow building with two rooms up and downstairs, the two doors facing Perry Street, and was painted gray. In the middle 1870's the primary room was divided and, in 1880, the building was remodeled, two rooms and halls being added on the west side and the original upstairs room made into an auditorium. The building was razed after the flood of 1937 and the present one erected.

Above the school stood the small store and a cottage of Christian Kinsler, and next to it the two-story frame home of the George Pratt family. This was razed and the lot has remained vacant for many years. Above Laurel Alley are three houses, the corner occupied in the 1870's by the S. H. Walcott home. On the northeast corner of Laurel Alley stood the Heisler Furniture Store, which was moved to the corner of Main and Laurel in the 1880's. Mr. Heisler was the only undertaker in the town for many years. On the northwest corner stood the brick North Methodist Church, razed when the churches united.

West of the Methodist Church corner stood the Russell Moran cottage, now the site of a storage building, and the brick house built in 1880 by the Kinsler family, the latter house looking as it did in those early days. On the corner of Perry and Harrison is a very old one-story frame building which, in the 1870's and later, was kept by a French woman known to the school children as "Mrs. Fred." As I remember her best she wore a very large hoop skirt and gold hoop earrings. She later married Albert Shilling, a shoemaker, and ran a restaurant on Washington Street. The frame building between the corner mentioned and the Pfaff corner was built by Joseph Pfaff in 1883 as a recreation hall for the young people of the town. Since that time it has housed the post office, printing offices and restaurants. The one-story building on the corner of Main and Harrison Streets was built by Joseph Pfaff in the 1860's for a residence and tailor shop.

On the present bank corner stood the brick home of John Mackoy in the 1870's. A brick store building was later erected on the site. The Stevens-Pollock, later Biggs-Lawson, Hardware Store stood next, and then the Dr. A. G. Drugstore, the Dickey-Hoop Shoe Store, and the John Bierley Bakery occupied the space extending to Elizabeth Street. This frame bakery is built on the site of the general store of Jehu Sydenstricker, which burned in the early 1870's. The brick building on the opposite corner was built by Amos Thornsbury who moved to Texas in the late 1870's, and the building has housed printing shops and lawyers' and doctors' offices since. The Joseph Pollock Bank occupied the present site of the Fire Department.

The Dr. William S. Kouns Drugstore occupied the frame building next to the bank. The remainder of Harrison Street to Lot 13 at the corner was occupied by a row of shops until in the early 1880's, when Nicholas Bergmeyer built the hotel later operated by the Patton family. Only one of these shops, now used for an office, remains.

The Kouns House was built by Major John C. Kouns in 1827 and he kept a tavern there until in the 1840's, when the John Winn family took it over and operated it until recent years. The original brick part of this building is still in use by descendants of the Kouns-Winn family. On the original yard a block house has been erected and has been used for a restaurant.

Above the Kouns House stands the brick house that was built before 1820 by Sam Seaton for a residence and a store. This was the home of the Dr. Alfred Spalding family for many years. Dr. Spalding died in 1878, and later the family moved to New York, where two sons, George and Alfred, were practicing physicians. This property became the home of the Alvin Morton family, where members of the family resided until the 1937 flood when it was badly damaged. When repaired it was used as a public building until the present courthouse was constructed. It is now owned and occupied by the Applegate family.

The brick house adjoining the above-mentioned property was built by the Allen Myers family about 1820, and only members of the family have occupied it. The present owner is Loretta Myers, who has furniture made by the original Allen Myers, who was a cabinet maker, in the shop on the corner of the lot which is still in use by a member of the family. The square from the corner of Front and Harrison Streets to Laurel Alley, where once stood the frame house of Martin Morris, is a frame house that was built by Dr. A. G. Sellards who sold it to Dr. A. S. Brady when he moved to Portsmouth in 1893. It is now owned and occupied by Dr. H. H. Holbrook as a home and office. The brick house above was also built by Dr. Sellards in the late 1870's, and was the Monroe Webb home for many years. The large brick house on the corner of Front and Hickory was built by Mr. George T. Halbert, who also built a frame office building on the lot below it, which was moved farther to the rear and made into the present dwelling house. The Halbert family removed to their former Vanceberg home and the residence built changed owners many times until bought by William A. Biggs, whose family resided there until recently.

Across Hickory Alley stands a brick house built by the John C. Kouns family, probably in the 1840's, which was sold to Archer Womack in the 1860's. It has been the property of the Owen Kendall family for a number of years. The two-story frame house above was owned and occupied by the Dr. Alfred DeBard family, and was built about 1869 or early 1870's. The frame office, later a school room, has been removed from the lower side. The very old McCoy cottage was razed some years ago and the site is vacant. Very recently the house on the corner of Front and Boston Alley (now Ash Street), a two-story frame, was razed. This was built in 1871 by John Russell, sheriff, and changed owners often until bought by A. L. Reid, whose family occupied it for a greater length of time.

Across Boston Alley (Ash Street) stands a two-story frame house that for a long time was the Van Dyke-Pollock home and is now the property of Mr. and Mrs. F. H. Forsythe. This, a one-story house when built by Charles Wilson, a furnace man, was changed to its present form by A. C. Van Dyke. The James D. Atkinson and Harry Curry homes have been built on the A. C. Van Dyke lawn. Above these stood a cottage owned and occupied by the

James R. Sowards family, which has been moved by them to the rear of the lot, facing Elizabeth Street. On Town Branch, at the head of Front Street, stood the Myers mill, which was later bought and operated by Robert Wilson, Sr. This burned in the late 1880's and was rebuilt by Sowards-Wilson, in 1889, on Harrison and Railroad Street.

The John C. Kouns homestead at the head of Elizabeth Street was the home of the descendants, Hollingsworth and Sands families, before and after the three decades. The Dr. John Sowards family bought and occupied the home later; it is now the Edward Hoffman home. Below this were two cottages on Elizabeth Street, homes of the Harvey Hodges and of the James Worthington families. The McCubbin home is built on the Hodges lot, and the Worthington lot is vacant.

The square between Jefferson Street and Boston Alley contains six lots, and besides the two mentioned were two cottages built by Mrs. George Callihan and by John Hollingsworth, and below these, in the 1870's, stood two very old cottages, that were occupied by Adam Frye and by a lawyer named Filson who did not remain very long in the town. The two-story frame homes belong to the Kendall and Kinner families. The one on the corner has changed owners several times since it was the William I. Myers property.

Across Boston Alley (Ash Street) stands a very old house built by George Roe, a lawyer. The lot below it remained vacant until about 1880, when the Benjamin F. Pratt family built the present house. The Pratt family moved to Cincinnati and the B. F. Lacock family operated a hotel there during the 1880's. This became the property of the Joseph B. Bennett family and is now the property of the Methodist Church. This church was built in 1845, on Lot No. 27, donated by the Kouns family. It had originally two front doors. An addition has been built on the rear in recent years.

On the east corner of Main and Hickory stands a two-story frame house which was the home of the Charles Hertel family and later of the Downs family. Across the alley is a modern house built by J. Watt Womack and the Stennett family. It stands where the cottage of Charity, the Negro servant of Edward Dulin, once stood. The Dulin home, a two-story frame house, was occupied during the decades by Edwin Dulin, his sister Mrs. Mary Dickey, and her two sons Charles and Ollie. The house below it was originally a Pratt home and later the home of the Manlius White family. Originally a cottage, it was made into its present form in recent years.

The George Childerson cottage, later the David Mitchell home, has been razed and the present brick home and office of Dr. Charles Conley was erected on the site. On the rear of this lot stands a block building that housed a grocery operated by the Kinner family and is now occupied by Frank Meadows with Ashland Oil Company. Across from this building is a one-story block building that houses the *News* office and those of the lawyers J. B. Bates and L. E. Nicholls. On the west corner of Main and Laurel once stood a building occupied by a store and the home of the David Mitchell family in the 1870's. A filling station now occupies this corner.

Below the corner building is a brick house that was built by John Hoffman in the early 1880's for his home and shop. This is now occupied by a drugstore and a restaurant. Below this building stands the Christian Church, built in the 1940's on the site of the original church that was built in 1855. Next to the church stood a very old two-story frame house which was the James Winters home in early days. It was razed in the 1890's, and the Columbia Hotel was built on the site. The Ireland home, later the home of the John Mackoy family stood on the corner of the present Russell-Greenup Bank.

On the opposite corner stands a one-story frame building built in the 1860's by Joseph Pfaff, a tailor. Frame buildings above the Pfaffs' were occupied by the shoe shop of Jacob Thornsbury, by the Adam Frye tin shop, and at one time by the post office. The next cottage was occupied by the Charles Reid family before they moved to Texas in 1880's. Above this stood the John Moran home and brick store. The store housed the post office, with Mr. Moran postmaster, from 1872 to 1882. The brick buildings, housing a furniture store, the Lawson Hardware, and a grocery, have been erected since the beginning of the present century. Near the corner of Main and Laurel is a building that was occupied by a millinery store, and by the Hertel-Eifort General Store in the 1870's-1880's. Much later it was occupied by the Taylor and Schmutz Grocery.

Across Laurel Alley stood the very old home of the Heisler family. This was razed and the present building was moved from the rear of the lot. The original Hertel home above this lot has been razed and the McCubbin building erected on the site. A house built by Sebastian Eifort in the 1860's, which was owned and occupied by the Edward Womack family for many years, has been razed and is used for a parking lot. Also, the Charles Van Bibber home on the corner built in the middle 1870's, has been razed and the lot is vacant. On the opposite corner stood the cottage of Dr. John Sellards, where now stands a building that was built by Charles Taylor, who ran a picture show. The first telephone exchange was located in the Sellards home with Rose Sellards as operator.

The Biggs Motor Company now occupies the lot where the brick house of Amos Thornsbury was built in early days. After changing owners several times it became the property of Mrs. Pansy Fullerton. The next lot, which was occupied by the Johnny Myers home, was razed, and the present building on the lot is the property of Charles B. Bennett. This was the home of the C. W. Mytinger family. The large frame house on the corner was built by Edward (Bud) Roe when he married Miss Agnes Barklow. He did not live very long to enjoy it. It is now owned and occupied by the C. B. Bennett family.

Across Boston Alley (Ash Street) stands the Thomas Wilson home, built in the 1870's and occupied since by only members of the family. The Bertis Smith home stands on the site of the Nelse Jackson house. The lot once occupied by the Sanford Hurn family is vacant. The land between this lot and the corner was vacant for a long time. Members of the John Moran family built the two cottages in the early 1900's. A filling station occupies the corner. At the head of Main Street facing Jefferson is an ornate house built by Nicholas Bergmeyer in the 1890's. It was bought by the David Downs family and later by the Nicholas Cline family. It is the property of a church group.

At the rear of the town beyond the Chesapeake and Ohio Railroad stands the old home of the William S. Kouns family of the three decades. For many years this was the home of the William Cole family, and later of the Sam Leslie family. Below this are three large frame houses, which were built by Scott, Matt and Denny Warnock. The one built by Scott Warnock is the property of the Edward Womack family. The other two belong to members of the Warnock families.

XIV

Childhood Memories

THIS STORY of childhood days contains much about my Grandmother S——, the only grandparent whom we children ever really knew—but she must have been all-sufficient, for we did not miss any of those we might have known if circumstances had been different. This seems strange to me as I look back, since I knew other children who had several.

Grandmother, then a very young girl, had come with the family from Virginia to Kentucky in the early 1800's. She was supposed to remain in Virginia with members of her mother's family until later. She owned a pony and was permitted to ride "a piece of the way" with her family. She never turned back but came on to Greenup County.

Her parents bought a small farm where the nine children grew to manhood and womanhood. She taught country schools and married a farmer who died in the early 1840's, leaving five young daughters. In a few years she remarried and three more daughters were born. The older daughters married while the family lived on the farm and the remainder of the family, Grandfather, Grandmother, the three young daughters, Aunt Sukey and three children, leaving other Negroes on the farm, came to the small town on the Ohio River. Grandfather bought a large old house, built in furnace days, also the store, which, with other buildings, yard and gardens, occupied a square fronting on the river. Grandfather went away at the beginning of the Civil War and never returned, and Grandmother, with the help of Aunt Sukey, managed the house and store, the latter until 1870.

During the war years the three young daughters married, the oldest leaving and the twins remaining in the home for the greater part of their married lives. It was home to us children, who grew up in that lovely place—more like brothers and sisters than cousins. The old-fashioned house had a yard of fruit trees with swings, as well as apples, damsons, dark red cherries, a large pear tree and a very large old tree that Grandmother said was an apricot and which, occasionally, bore a fruit like a large red plum. There were General Jack and Maiden Blush roses and a lilac that had been trained as a tree, so high that we children climbed up on an old-fashioned board fence to reach the blooms. Grandmother kept a cow and several pigs, raising the corn to feed them. This gave us some knowledge of her country life on the farm when our mothers were children.

As we grew older we learned about our other grandparents, of the grandmother who had died when my father was a young boy and of the grandfather who came to visit us in the early 1870's on his way to another son's home in Illinois.

In the 1880's, while I was teaching a country school not far from where my great-grandmother lived with a daughter, I went to the home to visit her. She was the mother of my grandfather who had gone away from home during the war. My Great-aunt Mary took me to her room, where she was bedfast. She raised up in her bed and talked to me, but called me by my mother's name. She was over one hundred years old at that time. In later years I visited the family graveyard and read on her headstone, "Born 1779, died 1889."

I recall that when I was a little girl I heard my mother and Aunt Betty talking together and laughing about something that had occurred when their father was still at home. They were just beginning to have beaus and he grumbled a great deal about it. One day when two young gentlemen came to call, he was very polite and entertained them until the young ladies should appear, which they never did. They couldn't be found, having climbed out of a window onto the kitchen roof that was covered thickly with vines and hidden. It was a lesson that he did not soon forget.

Grandmother was the most patient person that I ever knew, and though she had troubles hard to bear, I never saw her angry. When deeply disturbed she would breathe a deep sigh, go into her room and close the door. No one intruded for we knew she was talking it over with her Lord. Grandmother was a great reader, her favorite being the *New York Ledger* with the stories by Mrs. E. D. E. N. Southworth. She always kept a green-covered almanac handy, planting her garden according to the signs of the moon. This contained Franklin's maxims and other interesting material. Reversing the old saying about Jack, Grandmother believed that all play and no work was not good for anyone. One spring she gave each of us a small bit of her garden and seeds to plant. I do not remember what the other children raised on theirs but mine produced something that none of us children had ever seen and which Grandmother told us were pomegranates. They smelled delicious, and Grandmother liked them.

Sometimes we went to Grandmother's room before bedtime and she told us stories of her life when she was a little girl in Virginia and of the journey to Kentucky of which we never tired of hearing. Our earliest knowledge of the Bible was learned through the stories she made so interesting, of the children of Israel's journey from Egypt, of the Golden Calf made from their gold jewelry, of Jonah and the whale, Daniel in the lion's den, and of the three boys in the fiery furnace. When she began the last, we knew it meant bedtime, for she always ended it with Shadrach, Meshach, and "To bed we go."

She often quoted Franklin's sayings, one of which, "Dirty hands make clean money," puzzled me a great deal. She showed us how to make what she called a touch button, giving each of us a string with a large button tied on one end, which if touched the owner was entitled to a button. It may have been a button-saving device but we became such enthusiastic collectors that we sometimes had to "unstring" for a needed button.

While we children had many happy times, there were others not so, as at one time when five of Mother's and four of Aunt Betty's had the measles at one time and a little sister took them later and died, which was the first real grief we had known. Aunt Sukey helped to care for us and wanted us dosed with sheep tea, but mother thought hot toddies would be more pleasant. I didn't know until much later what sheep tea was made of. When a small child I was subject to phthisic and wheezed very loud, especially at night. While Mother greased a cloth with lard and turpentine, Father gave me some medicine with brown sugar on a spoon, which produced an upheaval of phlegm. I have never liked brown sugar since. One winter when I had an unusually lengthy spell of phthisis, Father taught me to spell phthisis, phlegm and wheeze, words I never forgot. Every so often my father thought the family needed medicine and would make a large glass pitcher of lemonade, which looked so good that we did not mind the Epsom salts that was included. One time there was an epidemic in the town and many children wore small bags of asafetida around their necks. The school room did not smell like a rose that winter.

Two incidents of my childhood memories concern warts, things we never hear of anymore. When we came home from Sunday school, a small cousin and I went to a swing in the yard to talk about it, I suppose. She had a wart on the lobe of her ear and said, "I wish I didn't have this wart on my ear." Some little classmate had probably mentioned it. I said, "Do you want me to take it off?" She said, "I wish you could." So, "thumb and finger went to work." I must have pinched pretty hard for not only the wart but such a quantity of blood ran down over her pretty Sunday dress that we both ran into the house, where our mothers took over. The wart was gone for good.

The other incident occurred much later. I had a ring that I could not wear on the proper finger because of not only one but two seed warts. I must have been in an unusually bad humor one day when Louisa, the Negro washwoman, brought the clothes, for she asked my mother what was the matter with me. Mother told her about the ring and the warts. Louisa said, "You get you a piece of brown paper like the store man wraps fat meat in, rub the warts with it and lay it folded out on the street." I did as she said and, strange to say, I forgot about the warts until one day I picked up the ring, put it on the finger and there were no warts to prevent. They were gone entirely and to this day, I believe that Louisa "charmed" the warts off.

When we children were old enough to do chores and run errands, one of our most pleasant ones was to go to the drug store. Dr. Kouns would give us a piece of licorice root or a cake of tolu to chew. The tolu was something new, as the only kind of chewing gum we had known was flavored paraffine.

All of our chores were not so pleasant as going to the drug store, as I remember Mother telling my older sister to do something and she told me to do it and I promptly relayed the chore to my younger sister. Mother looked at us a minute and said, "You remind me of the Jones family who lived in the country near us when I was a little girl and who had five boys. When Tom was told to do a chore, he said, 'Let Jim do it,' and he said, 'Let Bill do it,' and he said, 'Let Ben do it,' and he said, 'Let Pete do it,' and as Pete was the last one it ended with little Pete doing all the chores." And Mother added, "Pete was the only one that amounted to a hill of beans." By this time we were all willing to do the required chore and we never forgot the Jones boys.

Appendix

1957-1960

June 1957—The Chesapeake and Ohio Realty Company, with headquarters at Huntington, purchased land lying between the C. & O. right of way and the Ohio River at Frost. This embraced a part of the King, Biggs and Robinson, and all of the Hitchcock and Holbrook, farms. Other land at Frost owned by R. O. Judd and William Lawson was sold in 1956 to the above-named company.

December—South Shore was incorporated, taking in land lying one-half mile on both sides of Highway U.S. 23 and one-half mile wide. It also annexed the surrounding area that included a part of Fullerton.

A branch of the Russell First and Peoples Bank was established at South Shore.

1958—After fifty years of the production of its product, the King Powder Plant at Wurtland discontinued operations. Workmen are razing the buildings that were used by the plant.

After many years of service fifteen post offices in the rural districts of the county have been discontinued with fourteen remaining. Three rural routes have been established: Flatwoods, Greenup and South Shore.

1959—A court record of January, 1859, reads, "Ordered that W. E. Ireland, Lewis Ross and George Roe be appointed to buy a poor farm for the county, to pay $1,000, and the land not to be more than ten miles from the courthouse." The land was bought at Wurtland and a frame house constructed.

One hundred years after the above was done, the property at Wurtland has been sold and a modern home built at Smith Branch for the care of the poor.

A radio station, WIOI, was opened near the mouth of Tygart Creek on land purchased from Mr. and Mrs. Forrest

King. The station equipment includes a 250-foot tower with RCA transmission at Kings Addition with a studio and office at South Shore. S. M. Sinyard of Birmingham, Alabama, is president, and his brother, J. D. Sinyard, of St. Augustine, Florida, manager and engineer.

The bypass at the rear of Russell has been completed.

January 1960—Engineers have begun the construction of a reservoir on Little Sandy in Carter County. The construction of a reservoir on Tygart Creek at Kehoe, in Greenup County, has been deferred.

The old dam at Greenup has been closed. The new lock is being used upstream by heavy traffic, while other traffic may choose between the wall on the Kentucky side or the coffer dam on the Ohio.

A model built by the Huntington District engineers shows how a highway bridge could be built across the top of the Greenup high lift dam to link Kentucky and Ohio. The piers were constructed so as to carry such a span. William D. Newling is the resident engineer.

Jesse Stuart, West Hollow poet, writer and novelist has accepted a position as teacher at the University of Cairo and with his family will leave in July for that city, where he plans to remain a year.

One hundred years ago the northeastern part of Greenup County became Boyd County. It was named in honor of Linn Boyd, a prominent member of the Kentucky General Assembly and a member of Congress who, during the 1850's, was identified with much of the federal legislation of the pre-Civil War period.

February—Eight hundred names were stricken from the county list of voters by a committee appointed November, 1959.

The A.E.P. (American Electric Power Company), purchased eight hundred and seventy-eight of the one thousand acres owned by the King Powder Company of Wurtland. It is to be used by the Franklin Real Estate Company, a subsidiary of the A.E.P.

March—The snow that began with a storm February 18 will long be remembered. With continued snowfalls and flurries the ground was covered to a depth of from ten to eighteen inches in many places until March 24. The new bypass at Russell suffered two serious slides during the snow period.

April—A new high school will be constructed for Russell District on the south side of Powell Lane in the Kenwood-Flatwoods Section. Jesse Stuart, poet-novelist, has turned over a collection of his original manuscripts to Murray College at Murray, Kentucky. It was while giving a lecture in the auditorium of Murray College, October 8, 1954, that he suffered the heart attack which caused a serious illness of several months.

1960—The new Greenup post office building on the corner lot at Perry and Laurel Streets was finished according to schedule.

1961—The Columbia Gas Company has built a plant on the land bought by the C. & O. R.R. at Frost.

A plastic brick plant has been built at Siloam.

The Hooker Company of New York is building a plastic plant, also at Siloam.

March—from the *Greenup News* of March 18, 1960, we take the following county census figures from 1810-1960.

1810 — 2,369	1890 — 11,911
1820 — 4,311	1900 — 15,432
1830 — 5,852	1910 — 18,475
1840 — 8,297	1920 — 20,062
1850 — 9,654	1930 — 24,554
1860 — 8,760	1940 — 24,917
1870 — 11,463	1950 — 24,887
1880 — 13,371	1960 — 29,238

Towns

Greenup	1,240	South Shore	658
Russell	1,458	Bellefonte	337
Flatwoods	3,741	Raceland	1,115
	Worthington 1,235		

General Index

Conclusion

As THERE will be no more printings of *A History of Greenup County*, we have compiled this Supplementary Edition especially for those who may not have obtained one of the earlier books. We have included in this smaller and less expensive history many of the important facts contained in the others.

We have included material that has accumulated, of the town and surrounding areas of the decades 1870-1880-1890, childhood and school days, as we knew them. We have used no reference notes but have endeavored to give credit where due.

We thank all who have shown appreciation of *A History of Greenup County,* and also those who have aided us in the compiling of this Supplementary Edition.

THE AUTHOR